Mystic Saints of India: 2

CHAITANYA MAHAPRABHU

B.K. Chaturvedi.

Series Editor: Dr. Mahendra

BOOKS FOR ALL

DELHI-110052

Distributed By:
D K Publishers Distributors P Ltd.
1, Ansari Road, Darya Ganj, New Delhi-110002
Phones: 3278368, 3261465 Fax : 3264368
visit us at: www.dkpd.com
e-mail: dkpd@del3.vsnl.net.in

First Published 2000
ISBN 81-7386-223-0

Published By:
Books For All
B-2, Vardhaman Palace,
Nimri Commercial Centre,
Ashok Vihar Phase-IV, Delhi-110052
Phone: 7401672, 7452453
visit us at: www.lppindia.com
e-mail: lpp@nde.vsnl.net.in

Printed At:
D K Fine Art Press P Ltd. Delhi

SERIES' EDITOR'S NOTE

In 1963, Dr. Radhakrishnan, the President of India, declared in Bombay, " The time has come for all countries to work towards making the world a single home for Humanity.....Economics, Politics and transport have done their jobs. But we have to do as to give a soul to the world which has found a body, you can give it if you are truly Indian." We Indians are proud to have so many mystic saints in our history who can contribute the upliftment of the human being.

In Indian thinking, there are two modes in which we acquire knowledge: Argument and Experiment. Both these modes, together with experience play an important role in the development of mankind. Saints of India, through their arguments, tried to communicate their experiences to human beings. The represent an adventure in thinking.

This series, it is hoped, will enable the reader, eastern or western, to understand and appreciate currents of Indian thoughts by depicting the life and writings of different saints, we have tried to portray the true picture of Indian culture. I am really thankful to all those, who have helped in preparing and publishing these books, as it will not only propagate the ideas of Indian saints, but also help in making the mankind a better race.

Our world, becomes wider, our imagination richer and our life more colourful and more gestful as the result of our companionship with these saints, who are the travellers of the spirit and the pioneers of thought.

25.7.99 **(DR. MAHENDRA)**

Contents

Preface

Chaitanya Mahaprabhu is one of those luminaries in the firmament 'Pure Devotion' whose shine can never fade because what he inspired was pure love. He also introduced a novel way of achieving it: the Sankirtan or group singing or chanting one holy string of words for collective concentration. No matter how materialistic the world may become the element of yearning for union of coalescence with the Maker can not be eliminated from human life since it is natural. This renowned medieval saint from Bengal only revived the dormant yearning in the human consciousness.

The attempt in this work has been to cover Chaitanya from all angles. What were the conditions of Bengal when he was born, why Bhakti in that era become so rampant, how Chaitanya rose from being a delinquent prankester to such a noble saint are some of the questions that have been answered with an impartial analysis in this book, particularly in the backdrop of the present times which badly require a guileless heart to get to peace of union of coalescence.

The author is grateful to all those authors whose books could provide him the relevant material to make this work a useful study of Chaitanya and of the literature related to him, for which he is indebted to his friend Dalip Mukherji. Also, he express his gratitude to Mittal Brothers of 'Books for All' who have been a great help to him. May the tribe increase.

B.K. Chaturvedi.

I. Chaitanya Mahaprabhu

Devotion Personified

Among the various ways that the scriptures ordain for reaching the ultimate one of them is path of Bhakti or devotion. The word Bhakti is derived from the root Bhaj, which literally means 'to serve' or 'to adore'. One of the interpretations of this term claims that a 'Bhakta' is that entity which is separated from the whole and its ultimate object is to merge itself with that whole. Hence Bhakti requires total surrender of the self with the chosen Lord. Like the rivers have only one aim : to merge their entity with the Sea, so the path of Bhakti means total merger of the soul (Atma) with Supreme Being (Param-Atma).

Bhakti and Upasana mean much the same. Bhakti implies faith in the personal God, loving him and dedicating everything to his service. Although the path of knowledge also has the same aim, the difference between realisation of the ultimate truth the Bhakti Marg and Gyan Marg is that the later knows whither one is going the former claims that where the path is leading to is one's ultimate destination. In this way while Shankaracharya is the blatant example of the one following the path of knowledge, Chaitanya Mahaprabhu is the ultimate example of path of Bhakti. While Gyan may have discernment , which makes the merger somewhat difficult, Bhakti demands total surrender – negation of the self even while retaining the identity. Like Goswami Tulsidas claims :

Tehi jānahu jehi deu janāyee
Jānat tumhahi tumhahi hui jāyee

Meaning : He knows you whom you allow to be known and knowing you he becomes you yourself?

Thus devotion finds its fulfilment in complete self-surrender. Devotion, therefore, is the key-note of the creed of Vaishnavism[1] of which Chaitanya is the most brilliant example. The followers of the Bhakti Marg (path of devotion) often argue in its favour that of the paths, that of knowledge and that of devotion the latter is the easier of the two. The Bhagwat Gita says that for a person who

[1]Follower of Lord Krishna; this forms one of the three prominent sects of Hinduism. The other two being Shaiva (follwers of Lord Shiv) and Shaakta (follower of Goddess Shakti). Those who follow all the sects are called 'Smaarta' i.e. the follower of the intrepretation or the Smriti.

has been endowed with a human body, the Advait path of knowledge is difficult. The reason for the Bhakti-marg being easier is because it fills the devotee's mind with peace and great ecstasy.

But is devotion really the easier way? In a way it is and in a way it isn't. Knowledge can be gained by its constant pursuit. But devotion can not be got in this manner. It requires a purity of the mind and heart, a certain kind of nature (swabhāva) in which there is humility, love, freedom from jealousy and envy, and an inclination towards the divine. It needs total negation of the self. As the scripture claim three attributes are rather inseperable from one's personality : 'mamtā' (infatuative affection) 'ahamtā' (ego or I-sense) and 'vasanā' (passion). Of these three one can root out 'mamtā' and 'vasana' but 'ahamtā' is very difficult to obliterate. Even the most renowned seers who had renounced this entire world could not obliterate the sense of I-less. Otherwise there should have been no reason for their developing conflict among themselves. In fact any conflict arises out of difference of opinion and this difference results because each one has one's individualised thrust on a particular issue. And unless I-ness is not obliterated completely from one's personality one cannot be a true devotee. So despite one having all the required attributes if one remains conscious of the self one can't attain perfection on this path of devotion. That is why even if one has the desired nature yet if God's grace is not forthcoming devotion will not be born. Hence in being a devotee God's grace is of greater importance than human effort. So while path of knowledge is open for all, devotion is for the chosen few. As Lord Krishna proclaims through the Gitā: "All beings are the same to me. I do not have any likes or dislikes. But those who worship me, I am in them and they are in me." Thus path of devotion is not that easy from two counts: it is difficult to root out one's I-ness and it is beyond your effort to ignite in you that divine spark all by your endeavour.

The Vaishnava cult believes that in order to achieve total self-surrender it is necessary to establish a close relationship with God. What that relationship is will depend upon the type of devotee. He may believe he is god's servant, comrade, child or beloved. Hence Bhakti path has been classified into many categories: like worship with sewā-bhāv (with total subservience), sakhā-bhāv (with a sense of comraderi) etc. But what distinguishes Chaitanya Mahaprabhu is his worshipping Lord Krishna with a feeling of total identity. Hence among the Bhaktimārg (followers of the path of devotion) he is peerless. Very rarely has a devotee dawned in the mortal world who claimed himself to be not only the devotee of Lord Krishna but Krishna himself. His this claim underlines his ardent desire to lose his identity and merge himself with the chosen Lord.

For Chaitanya, Krishna meant everything the existence is known by. He sought God in the form of Krishna. Like Gautama Buddha he also abandoned his home for a wider quest. His favourite mode of the expression of Krishna devotion was the 'Sankirtan' (singing the holy name accompanied by music and dance). He popularised this novel way of worship as much as to make him and Sankirtan inseperable. Although this tradition had been existing earlier also, it was Chaitanya who popularised it as much as to make it survive even to-day. Now this very tradition has spread much far and wide, even to the world at large. In fact the ISKCON or the Hare Rama, Hare Krishna movements have been its strong off-shoots only.

Chaitanya was a true ascetic after he become a Sanyāsi. In fact most of his time was spent in having communion with Lord Krishna.

Born so far away from the citadel of Krishan-bhākti i.e. Mathurā and Vraja region, in a village, Nâvadweep, in north Bengal, how this pioneer of the section of the Vaishnava cult could achieve so intense communion with Lord Krishna? How this renowned saint of the medieval period achieved his pinnacle: virtual coalescence with his chosen Lord are some of the questions which we shall be dealing with in the coming pages. Suffice it to say that very rarely such a homogenerous personality treads on the mundane earth whose action, thought and person could be so indistinguishable and all devoted to his merger of the self with Krishna.

II. Birth And Early Years

Chaitanya Mahaprabhu (1407-1533 A.D.), also known as Gaurang(of fair limbs) and popularly called Nimai, was one of the greatest saints of Vaishnava faith. He was born in Navadweep or Nadia, a village, on the banks of the Bhagirathi about seventy miles north of Calcutta. It was a famous centre of learning in medieval period and still a citadel of Vaishnavism. Before Chaitanya's birth there were many renowned scholars. One of them was Upendra Misra, a original resident of Sylhet district. He had later on, come and settled in Navadweep, drawn to this place by its renown for honouring the scholars. This Upendra Misra had seven sons, of whom Jaganath, was the fifth. Jaganath was very learned and very good looking. Hearing about his erudition and seeing his so appealing a personality, a learned Pandit of the region, Nilambar Chakravorti, gave his daughter, Shachi, in marriage to him. Though this pair produced eight daughters, none of them survived. Then on full moon night of the month of Phalgun, in 1407, a son was born to them exactly on the lunar eclipse day. As was the custom the people were then bathing in the holy river Bhagirathi with loudly chanting 'Hari Bol1! Hari Bol!' It was exactly at this moment, believed to be extremely auspicious by astrologers, that the child was born.

It is recorded by Lord Gaurang's biographers that when the child was born no sign of life was detected in the new born babe. Various means were adopted to revive him but for a considerable time without success. The boy, at last, began to breathe automatically and every one was delighted to hear the cry of the new born. The biographers also claim that the child was of an unusually large size since it was born having been full twelve months inside the womb.

Although officially the name given to the child was Vishambhar the women folk insisted on calling him Nimai. But when the Yogyopaveeta ceremony was held, because of his golden-yellow complexion he was also called 'Gaurang' (literally, of fair complexion). Finally, the name that boy came to be known to his followers with was Chaitanya which means fully conscious. The irony in the last name can't be missed because in his grown up stage he was often found unconscious to the material world since most of the time he was in communion with his chosen deity. But such enlightened or chosen souls have their own definition of conciousness. As Mirza Ghalib says:

Hai ghaib-ghaib jisko samajhate hain hum shuhood
Hain khwaab men hanoz jo jage jain khwaab main

[What we deem manifest is actually hidden since those who are dreaming dream feel as though they are conscious].

This is typically true in spiritual sense. If one is conscious for the divine existence one is necessarily asleep for the mundane world.

Nimai, as his mother called him, was a tall, healthy and strong child of great loveliness. He developed into a lively, live-wire-boy with an inexplicable peculiarity in him : Whenever he cried the mere mention of Hari would at once quieten him. This name seemed to have a magical effect on him right since the very beginning.

Many uncanny happenings have been recorded in his childhood. One day he caught hold of a cobra but it did him no harm. Another day a thief, Makh Mali, finding him alone and wishing to steal the gold bracelets he wore, carried him away. But as soon as the man seized the child a shudder went through him. It became evident to him that he was leading an evil life. Hurriedly he took the child back and left him at his father's house. Then, he relinquished the world and began to live an austere life. Ultimately he became a saint. Many supernatural incidents were seen by Nimai's parents Shachi and Jagannath. It was noticed by many that when Nimai slept, a moon-like radiance would emanate from his breast. The room would, at times, be filled with luminous figures. It is said that when he walked even bare-footed musical sounds like the jungle of anklets would be heard with the impression as if their source was his feet.

The boy was by nature restless. It was difficult to keep him under control. Often be would go out to play and return with his body covered with dust and grime and no matter he was warned every time he would make himself dirty. Also, he would ask every one for various things – parched rice, bananas, sweetmeats or whatever he saw. But uncontrollably charmed by his looks and captivating physique the people would grudge him nothing. The child would dance so enchantingly that people of the neighbourhood would offer him things to eat, just to see him dance and they would themselves feel irresistibly drawn to joining him in the dance, Nimai's graceful movements would enrapture the onlookers. Children would often make him dance while chanting 'Hari-Hari! Perhaps this passion for dance and music gave the fore signals of the Sankirtan to come in later years.

There was another peculiarity of him which is worthy of mention. It is said that he would pile up used earthen cooking pots and stand upon them. Since these were considered impure he was often asked by his parents to desist from doing so as the used pots were store house of filth and dirt, he would invariably say: "the idea of external purity is a delusion." Besides being unusual from one who was a mere child such an observation showed his broadmindedness and quite unique way of seeing things. This was the seed from which grew the characteristics of Chaitanya's faith which was totally non discriminatory and attached no significance to caste. Even as a child Nimai would touch even 'chamars' (those who dealt with leather and skin) whose touch was considered defiling. While he was not even five he began to weep uncontrollably one day and even the name of Hari, which usually quietened him, was of no avail. His desire this time was to eat the prasad (holy offering) which his neighbours Jagdish and Hiranya had prepared for Lord Krishna. Hearing the uproar the two brahmins came to find the cause, and when they saw the beauty of Nimai they began to suspect the boy-Nimai-to be an embodiment of Lord Krishna, and willingly gave him the sacred offerings. Shachi, the dotting mother found her son's these tantrums most unusual and sought the assistance of the ladies of the neighbourhood for she thought her son to be under the possession of evil spirits. By common resolve 'prasāda' was prepared to offer it to Shasthi (the protectress of children) but while Shachi was secretly taking the offering to the goddess, to her horror, Nimai got to know and snatching the 'prasāda' bolted with it. Since all the persons of Nawadweep were overcome with Nimai's ethereal loveliness no act of his, however mischievous, could annoy them. S.K. Ghose, in his "Gaurang or Salvation for All." describes Nimai's physical beauty on the basis of descriptions he had collected from original Bengali:

"A complexion resembling molten gold – The palms of his hands and the soles of his feet were, as it were, painted with fresh vermilion. When he ran about it seemed as if blood was oozing out of his feet. His features were beautifully formed. The counter of his body was simply perfect. The movement of every limb, the glance of his eyes, his smile and his face, free from the slightest defect, was, as it were, the master work of a sculptor of the highest genius. His tips were ruddy, like the ripe 'limba' fruit (which is red). But his eyes were perhaps more lovely than any part of his body. No one who had not seen the boy could believe that a human being could have eyes so divinely beautiful. His eyes elongated like the petals of a lotus slightly tinged with red seemed as if "moist with lotus honey".

When the boy Nimai came of age his all initial ceremonies like 'Karnabheda' (piercing the ear-lobes) and 'Chuda-karana' (at which bracelets are worn) were performed with due fanfare by his parents Jagannath and Shachi. As was the custom his education started from five years of age. Although not very precocious he had the innate ability to not only copy all the letters of the alphabet he could write out even compound letters with ease. He, however, derived extreme pleasure in writing the names of various incarnation of Lord Vishnu like Rama, Krishna and their epithets like Murari, Mukund or Vanmāli.

But school education didn't cease Nimai's typical tantrums. He would still ask for some impossible objects like the moon or the stars and would scream aloud at his not getting them. Then invariably the chanting of 'Hari's name would quiten him. Moreover, his playing all kinds of pranks and mocking at other boys were continuing unabated which frequently led to fights. But he would always manage to fox the other boys. Pouring water over the head of innocent persons meditating quietly on the bank of the river, spitting upon those coming out of the river after bathing, dragging the legs of people half immersed in the water performing the 'Sandhyā' ceremony are some of those highly disturbing pranks. When he started switching on the clothes of the male, the female bathers, the people decided enough was enough and reported the matter to his parents. But meanwhile Nimai very tactfully sprinkled some drops of ink on his clothes to prove that he had been to the school. In fact Nimai's all pranks were to those that according to Bhagvat Purana and other religious books were also performed by Lord Krishna in the childhood.

Nimai's elder brother, Vishwaroopa, was ten years senior in age to him. Now when Nimai was six years old, he was sixteen, Vishwaroopa had attached himself to Advaita and was a serious minded scholar. Nimai was greatly attached to him. On being forced to marry Vishwaroopa deserted the house. He died two years later at Pandharpur near Pune. This event cast a serious effect on Nimai's psyche. Vishwaroopa's departure was also a calamity for Jagannath can Shachi. After this event Nimai was a changed boy and he assured his parents that he would look after them. Thenče forward he became extremely studious and serious minded boy.

After his elder brother's departure Nimai began to fare very well at school. Jagannath feared that if Nimai too became as great a scholar as his brother was, he too might leave the world and become an ascetic. With this apprehension in mind he removed him from the school. But this precaution had a retrograde effect, and Nimai again resumed his pranks along with his unruly companions. One day he went and sat on the heap of discarded mud pots. His fare body was streaked with soot. Shachi was aghast and scolded him for touching impure things. Then the boy shrewdly retorted: "how could you expect me to have this discernment when I am deprived of education." The he added rather pompously "nothing can make me impure. Whichever object I touch becomes pure. The pots in which Vishnu's offerings have been cooked can never be impure." Shachi was afraid that should Jagannath know about his pranks and arguments he might be enraged. But the neighbouring ladies who heard Nimai's arguments supported him while wondering that whereas all other lads resented their going to school, this was a different lad who was so adamant to rejoin the school. Ultimately the matter was brought to the notice of Jagannath who eventually agreed with Niami.

When boy Nimai was nine, arrangements were made to hold the sacred thread (Yagyopaveeta) ceremony. Unlike other places, in Nadia the custom was the father's breathing the holy 'Gayatri Mantra' into his son's ear. As soon as Jagannath did so the boy fainted away with a scream. Tears rained from his eyes and his body shone with an effulgent light. Describing the event S.K. Ghose says: "When, after sometime his mother saw him, Nimai's divine appearance awed him. Addressing her he said, 'I am leaving this body. I shall come again. The body I am leaving behind is your son's, whom you should look after with great tenderness when I am gone. Thereafter the boy became unconscious and appeared dead. A few moments after the hallow which had surrounded his head vanished and Nimai come to his natural state, much to the mother's relief!"

It was during one of those days that Jagannath dreamt one day that his one son had become a monk and had developed a large number of followers. It disturbed him so much that he got up with a start and told Shachi about it who assured her husband that dreams were unreal. Little did she realise how wrong she would be proved by future. Soon after this incident Jagannath got an attack of fever which proved fatal. While unaware of the approaching calamity Nimai served him like a faithful son. Jagannath was pleased. Holding him close to his bosom he said:

"My son! I am going away with my desire unfulfilled. I leave you to God, my child. Pray not to grieve at my departure." With these words Jagannath expired Shachi was greatly shocked but Nimai comforted like a mature person. Yet Nimai's capriciousness continued unabated. With the earning member gone, the family was hard put financially. But unconcerned Nimai would demand whatever he wished at once. One day he insisted on getting a garland and sandal wood paste to worship Ganga after bath. When he was asked to wait for sometime he lost his patience and started breaking everything he could lay his hands on. Severely annoyed he rolled on the ground in a fit of rage. After his rage was spent Shachi gave him a bath and handed him the garland which now had come. Then Shachi gently reprimanded him saying that if he destroyed everything, how would their needs be fulfilled? Nimai laughed rather derisively, adding that "Krishna is the sustainer!" Then he left with his books to return after some time with two 'tolas' of pure gold! Giving it to his mother he said calmly: "My sustainer has given it. This shall suffice for the present. I told you 'he' is there to help us." But it remained mystery that from where that lad procured two 'tolas' of gold which in those time must have been a fortune!

When Nimai completed his studies he was 16, and soon he received an offer to teach a boy. He was invited by Mukund-Sanjay, who owned fabulous Chandimandap which was also kept at Nimai's disposal. In a short time many students began to attend Chaitanya's grammar school. Nimai had, by this time, become as accomplished scholar and he had a number of students in his charge. He would hold learned discussions with variours pundits and usually worsted them. Although he was still in his teens he started writing commentaries on sanskrit grammar which became popular in that region among the learned men. Afterwards he studied logics at a famous Nyāya school of Vasudeva Sarvabhauma. One of the teachers who also cooked food for the students, Raghunath, was particularly impressed by Nimai's clarity of thought. One day Vasundeva gave Raghunath a typical problem of logic. It was quite ticklish and Raghunath was quite involved in vain. One day Nimai found the food hour getting delayed so he came to enquire as to what was the problem. When Raghunath told him about the problem Nimai offered the solution there and then. It was during those days that Raghunath was working on the commentry on Nyaya. Nimai didn't know about it and he was also working on the same commentary. One day when they both wee strolling along the bank of the river Raghunath told him about his project. Nimai showed extra interest in that since that was the work he had also undertaken. When he told Raghunath about it and offered the samples of what he had worked on till then, Raghunath realised that his (Nimai's) work would prove superior to his. Crestfallen, Raghunath despaired and started crying. Nimai, realising the reason was so moved that he threw his entire manuscript in the river with an indifferent remark: "Nyāya, in any case, a fruitless philosophy!". From that moment he ceased to study Nyāya. Meanwhile Raghunath's commentary was out. Called as 'Didhit' it became the highest authority on the subject.

By this time Nimai was in his early twenties and his fame as a scholar had spread far and wide. Added to his erudition was his magnetic personality's charm and he became the centre of attraction of the region. So much so that before he entered his twentyfifth year a powerful monarch like Prataparudra, accompanied by his entourage of ministers and scholars, came to pay homage to him.

Perhaps this was the time when the learned Pundits of the region started suspecting Nimai having a divine spark. He had crossed the river Padma so as to bring his learning to the eastern districts. Some of his biographers also claim that this he did to collect donations for the institutions he was running. Whatever may be the case, this nobody denies that his tender age and wide erudition had made him quite renowned. One day a scholar, Keshava from

Kashmir, who had defeated every professor in every learned city of India (so it is claimed) came to Nadia with great pomp and show. He instantly composed more than a hundred couplets to impress Nimai with his ability and knowledge. But even hearing them once Nimai pointed out the defects in a few shlokas which were recited in the middle. Keshava was amazed that Nimai should in one recitation remember the particular couplets in between so many. It is mentioned by Chaitanya's biographers that ultimately the goddess Saraswati herself revealed to Keshava that the being who humbled his pride was none other that Lord Krishana himself. Then he also happened to meet Iswara Puri, a sannyasi and disciple of the celebrated Madhavendra Puri, said to be one of the most pious men of his age. The sannyasi at that time was involved in writing a book on the love of Radha and Krishna and at his request Nimai helped him in it. The sannyasi was amazed. But it seems till this time Nimai was not aware of his supernatural powers. But when he was revered by the learned scholars he was himself quite surprised since he was as playful as ever. His pranks were unabated, only their nature underwent a change. He would casually laugh and joke with his students. Though he dressed with exquisite taste-almost like a prince and looked every inch like the one – he had shed his vanity. Although behind his back other fellow scholars were jealous and called him proud and insolvent they did admit his intelligence. But unlike his childhood pranks now he was shy with women and girls.

III. Youth And Initiation

Not withstanding the transformation taking place in Nimai's nature and his getting increasingly shy and modest in the company of women, there was one exception. There was a girl called Lakshmi, his childhood companion, whom he frequently met while visiting the bank of Gangā. Nimai now was a full grown young man of irresistible charm and the renowned for his erudition. He had opened his 'Tol' (seminary). It was about this time he felt increasingly drawn to his childhood companion Lakshmi. Meanwhile, the pressure was on Nimai for getting married. A certain acquaintance of the family, Vanmali, then came to Shachi and suggested it was about time Nimai was married. He too suggested his marriage to Lakshmi, the daughter of Vallabhāchārya. She was quite beautiful and on all counts was an ideal match for Nimai.

However, Shachi was not very willing to accept this offer for her son. She first wanted Nimai to get well settled in life since he was the sole bread-winner in the family. As Vanmāli, who brought the offer, was going back he happened to meet Nimai and told him about the offer. He also said that Shachi was not that much willing to accept the offer. Though Nimai didn't say anything, when he reached home he did ask his mother as why didn't she pay due attention to Vanmāli. That hint was enough for Shachi. So when Vanmāli came next, she gave her consent to the offer he had earlier brought.

Meanwhile, Vallabhāchārya who had sent Vanmāli as his messenger to convey the offer was quite happy to give his daughter's hand to such a respected scholar. But he had also impressed upon Vanmāli that being poor he would not be able to give anything more that five 'Anwala fruit' (myrobalan fruit) as dowry. Since Shachi was not greedy for dowry she gladly accepted all that Vallabha promised to pay as dowry. Soon the marriage of Nimai with Lakshmi was solemnised without much fanfare. There was no pomp and show, and only a few relative and friends were invited. Shachi cleverly apologised that since not much time had elapsed to her husband's death she decided not to solemnise wedding on a grand scale. But her reference to Jagannath's death was enough to make Nimai sorely miss his father and he wept bitterly.

It appeared that following his marriage Nimai

became more conscious of his wordly duties. He became more engrossed in his profession. His would often say that those who did not know the 'rules of conjunction' (the first lesson in Sanskrit Grammar) became Sanskrit scholars in this Kali Age. The 'Vaishnava' were the target of his visit which was quite strange since he was to lead them in almost no time.

Despite being more circumspect and worldly, and a brahmin of high stature his innate trait of being friendly to other caste people did not desert him. He never despised or ignored other castes; even the lower ones, He would, without any inhibition, laugh and chat with lowly men like weavers, milkmen, small traders and so forth. They were so enamoured of this soft-spoken, charming person that whatever be wanted he received from them almost unasked. Thus he would wander about exulting in his knowledge, yet kind and affectionate to those low in the social reckoning, and holding animated discussions on the bank of Ganga with his students and other scholars. Yet at the same time he would continue passing witty remarks, jesting and taking time off for his hobbies like swimming. Following his visit to the districts across the river Padma, his reputation become all the more wide-spread. With the result his financial position also improved.

It was during this period a misfortune befell the family in Lakshmi's tragic death by snake-bite. Nimai was really heart-broken at the death of his wife. Although in those days there was not much interaction with wife in the traditional home yet Lakshmi by her devotion and care for her husband and mother-in-law had impressed both. But soon Nimai regained his composure and tried to dissolve his sorrow in devoting greater time to his chosen devotion – teaching. Now his routine was right from the day-break to noon he would take his class. On return a servant would put oil in his hair and give him a message. Afterwards he would go out and bathe in the Ganga, say his prayers and returning home take his meals and rest. In the evening he would go for a stroll along the river bank with his students and continue his discussion with them on a variety of philosophical subjects. Coming back home at the fall of night he would continue his reading till late in night.

Although he didn't express his longing for a wife, his mother felt much lonely after the death of Lakshmi. She was quietly on the look-out for a suitable girl for Nimai. She happened to find one quite easily. When she would go to the river to bathe she would often come across a very beautiful and modest girl whom she found invariably at the bank as if awaiting her arrival. And that girl would never miss greeting Shachi. In, return Shachi would always bless her saying: "May you get a good groom!" One day Shachi asked her name and was delighted to know she was Vishnupriya, the daughter of a rich and high caste brahmin of Nadia, Sanatan Misra. He was a renowned Pundit of that region. Although Sanatan belonged to the superior Gotra[1]" to that to which Nimai belonged when the proposal was made for marrying Nimai to Vishnupriya, Sanatan was more than willing being highly pleased with Nimai's charming personality and erudition. In fact he had set his eyes on making Nimai his son in law. Vishnupriya herself had conceived strong attraction for Nimai whom she had seen strolling on the bank of river in his simple majesty.

When Shachi broke the news to Nimai, he was immediately not very willing, being emotional by nature he valued still his demised wife's memory. But persuaded by his friends and well wishers, he agreed. His many friends and well-wishers were over-joyed and they happily announced to bear all the expenses of the marriage to be held on a grand scale. Eventually a Kayestha landlord, Buddhimanta Khan, bore most of the expenses.

So in his second marriage Nimai went to the bride's house accompanied by music, torches and fireworks and a

[1]Sub-division of a particular sect of Brahmin.

large number of friends and students. It is described that the couple looked strikingly matching in their wedding dresses. The two then were united in their matrimonial bliss. This wedding was celebrated with such gusto and flamboyance that it earned renown for many years as an incomparable marriage in the entire region. Nimai was also happy and Shachi was delighted to get such a noble and well mannered daughter in law. A few days after his second marriage Nimai engrossed himself again in his chosen profession: teaching.

The Initiation:

It was in the last phase of the year 1508 that Nimai went to Gaya to offer oblations to the departed soul of his father. As his luck would have it , there he accidentally met Ishwar puri again with his permission and guidance Nimai performed the holy rites . Then he requested Ishwarpuri to initiate him which the learned Pundit readily agreed. Prior to his requesting for initiation Nimai was greatly affected by the footprints of Lord Krishna – as it is generally believed in the temple at Gayā. For the one whom very mention of Lord Krishna's name was enough to throw into emotional ecstasy it was too much to behold any concrete symbol of that Lord. After seeing it he fell into a swoon and tears streamed from his eyes. It was

Ishwar Puri who lent a helping hand to prevent him from falling down. Then Inshwar Puri breathed in the ten bettered sacred Gopal-mantra "Gopivallabha pranamyate[1]" meaning "Salutation to the Beloved of the Gopis." While repeating the 'mantra' given to him he would suddenly fall into a state of ecstasy and lament loudly for Krishna. Then he decided to go to Mathura and asked his companions to return to Nadia without him. When he had moved only a little far suddenly he heard a divine voice saying: "It is not yet time to go to Mathura. You are the Lord to the world. Go home now and come to Mathura later."

Visit to Gayā and initiation by Ishwara Puri represent a major turning point in Nimai's life. It seemed God was guiding his destiny and had determined that now the time had come for bestowing his divine grace on one whom he had chosen to spread his message.

Many people feel amazed at God's choice to spread his message through Nimai, an arch oponent of the Vashnavites of his time. He used to make fun of Vaishnavas like Mukund and Shrivasa, so much that they avoided the proud pundit. In fact the choice of God for spreading his message is decided by purity of the intrument's heart. May

[1]Opinions vary about his mantra; the letters are counted according to Sanskrit sounds.

be such persons are apparently moving the wrong way but they have a guileless heart. They don't hide what they feel. History is full of such instances. In the Bible we are told that Saul was against Jesus's disciples and even went to the high priest to obtain orders that they be bound and produced before him. And as he was on his way to Damascus to bring the disciples when: "suddenly there shined round about him a light from heaven: And he fell to the earth, and heard a voice saying unto him, Saul, saul, why persecutes thou me? And he said who art thou Lord? And the Lord said, I am Jesus Whom thou persecutes: it is hard for thee to kick against the pricks."

Take, for instance the case of Swami Vivekananda. He was a votary of reason having no faith in ecstatic vision, which he considered to be mere hallucination, and being an agnostic with a scientific bent of mind. But just a touch of Shri Ramkrishna's hand transformed the non-believer into an enthusiastic Vedantist and worshipper of God. There are so many example to prove that it is not necessary that the strong devotee or votary of God may become the instrument to spread divine message. In fact we learn that most of the 'chosen' devotees were not extra-ordinary in any way. But if we closely analyse their lives we will find two main things in common: the desire for spirituality and purity of the heart. 'Sir Galahed' says:

"My strength is as the strength of ten
Because my heart is pure."
(Tennyson, 'Sir Galahad')

Thus the purity of heart is the prime requisite for being the divine messenger. The heart ought to be free of filth of every, rage, arrogance, hatred and so forth. Goswami Tulsidas in his celebrated 'magnum opus' 'Sriramacharitamānas' makes Lord Ram say:

"Nirmal man jan so mohi pāvā
Mohi kapat chhal chidra ma bhava

[I am accessible to only those whose heart is pure and guileless since I don't like deceitful and fraudulent persons]

This was precisely the case with Nimai. He had all the requisite qualities of a true devotee of the Lord but so long they were dormant–the straight forwardness, the purity of heart, the love for all men even the poor, out castes and the downtrodden. He never distinguished men on the basis of caste, creed and faith. All that was the reason why he was a recipient of the Lord's grace.

It was around Magh (Jaunary) 1509 that a changed Vishambhara (Nimai) returned to Nadia. His wife

Visnupriya was overjoyed, but as was the custom of the age, she stood bashfully behind the door and gazed from there on him. He went and bowed to his mother's feet. Neighbours, friends and relations all came to see him, for in those days undertaking a journey was fraught with risk and they all came to congratulate him on his safe return. But they all were rather surprised to meet a changed Nimai. He was no longer the happy go lucky, hilarious kind of person and had become serious minded. There was an unmistakable unearthly glow in him and he seemed to be in a spiritual state of communion with the divine. He was often found wailing for the Lord Krishna who would appear in a vision and disappear leaving him restless with his seperation and longing for reunion with him.

Seeing his condition her mother was rather alarmed. She had already lost her one son to ascetic order who had left home in the quest of God. She feared lest Nimai also should follow suit. Nimai was so much charged with a divine realisation that when his wife, Vishnupriya went near him, instead of greeting her conjugal love, he welcomed her with a flood of tears. The lady was frightened and ran to her mother-in-law in nervousness. When Shachi came, he was able to speak to her amid sobs and said in a emotion charged tone: "Be not afraid Mother! When I went to bed and was asleep I suddenly dreamt of a most beautiful

Being. Since then I am restless and it is difficult for me to control my tears." When he described that Being it was obvious that he dreamt of Lord Krishna.

This way Nimai continued to weep and wail whenever he thought of Lord Krishna. He was emotionally in an uncontrollable stage. While people were trying to make him become again reasonable and better controlled, another problem came before Nimai. His this stage had its worst impact on his tiny school (called 'tol' or seminary); for, now a scholar and a teacher was a changed man-an ardent devotee of Lord Krishna. Now the world had only one overpowring existence – for he found Lord Krishna wherever he looked. So instead of teaching his students the lessons he was always talking about Lord Krishna. After going on in this way he recollected himself , but unable to proceed left it at that, and promised to teach them the next day. But it was the same thing repeated. No doubt he was impressive and there was a serenity about him which was quite over powering, but the students had come for learning and in that, despite the long gap – because of their teacher's changed behaviour – they were not making any progress at all. Nimai felt totally helpless. Despite his realising that he was being unfair to his students he couldn't do anything about it. Many a time he made the resolve but each time any involuntary reference to Lord

Krishna made him swoon in ecstasy. At last he decided to do away with his 'tol' because it was impossible for him to continue with it. According to his biographer, S.K. Ghosh (as mentioned in his "Gaurang, Or Salvation for All") he called his students and addressed them the following way: "My friends, I will deal frankly with you, and reveal to you a secret which shouldn't be revealed to others. It is this: When I am about to teach you, at that moment a child of dark complexion and of exquisite beauty appears before me playing on his flute. The sight of him takes away my senses. Therefore, my dear friends, teaching you is out of my power, Nothing but Shri Krishna and matters concerning him come to my mind, my senses and my whole being have taken entire possession of by him. So, I freely give you leave to go wherever you choose for your education and may the blessing of Shri Krishna always attend you! Forget me not as I shall never be able to forget you all."

While saying so that young professor of twenty three was overcome with an uncontrollable emotion and tears began to flow down his cheeks. It was tearful farewell. Both the teacher and the students wept bitterly in a unique empathy. Then Nimai blessed the students individually. While announcing the closure of his seminary, Nimai taught each student a mantra before they parted for good. It was: “Hare namah Krishna-Yadava namh; Gopal Govind Rama Shri Madhusoodana.” Then the whole group song this mantra jointly. Describing the heart-rending farewell, S.K. Ghosh describes. “Gradually the external world began to grow dim and dimmer to their gaze – a holy joy filled their heart. Some laughed, some trembled, some rolled on the ground and some danced in exuberance of their feelings. The commotion in the ‘tol’ brought many spectators to the scene. They came as idle on lookers, but they too found themselves caught in the current before the preceptor who was them, as it were, “swimming in the river of Bhakti (devotion).” He was then one with has chosen Lord and what separated him was his physical entity. Little he knew that soon he was to realise what he actually was. The stage was set for His Revealing Himself.

was: "Hare naman Krishna-Yadava hari, Gopal Govind Rama Shri Madhusoodana." Then the whole group sang this mantra jointly.* Describing the heart-rending farewell, S.K. Ghosh describes: "Gradually the external world began to grow dim and dimmer to their gaze — a holy joy filled their heart. Some laughed, some trembled, some rolled on the ground and some danced in excess of their feelings. The commotion in the 'tol' brought many spectators to the scene. They came as idle on-lookers, but they too found themselves caught in the current before the preceptor, who was there, as it were, swimming in the river of Bhakti (devotion)." He was then one with his object of Love and what separated him was his physical entity. Little he knew that soon life was to realise what he actually was. The stage was set for His Revealing Himself.

IV. Divine Manifestation

After Nimai left teaching and closed his seminary he began to gather the Vaishnava devotees about him. This was the period marked by devotional sessions which began at Nimai's house and gradually shifting to other ardent Vaishnavites like Srivas, Chandrashekhar and others. It was during this very period that divine manifestation of the Lord (Krishna) were increasingly noticed through Nimai's person. Going by the descriptions available it is clear that such revelations came all of a sudden and lasted for varying periods – sometimes for a minute or even seconds and at times as long as a full day and night. When the Lord Krishna thus manifested himself he usually took the form of a divine light or effulgence of over powering brightness which surprisingly didn't dazzle the eyes as this kind of powerful light is supposed to dazzle. It was purely a divine light unseen on the earth. It was a brightness that was singularly devoid of any peering intensity.

At this juncture it is necessary to elaborate on this

kind of light. Modern research have confirmed that those who were 'clinically' declared dead 'yet life was revived in them later on also saw this kind of light.' These persons reported that their souls were confronted with a light of unearthly brilliance from which there emanated love and warmth truly ineffable. It is reportedly so beautiful and so bright, so radiant yet it didn't hurt the eyes. It is asserted that it was not any kind of light ever seen on the earth. It didn't actually see a person in this light and yet it has a special identity. It is a light to be seen and absorbed into your soul for its divine illuminations. It is that light in which the viewer, viewed and the observation all become one. Describing that divine light Jai Shankar Prasad describes in his classic of modern Hindi literature: 'KAMAYANI':

"That light of love prestine,
To all eyes there did bless
All looked recongnised in one
Phase of their one-ness
In harmony live-dead, all,
A beauteous form in appearance
Gleamed there one consciousness
Bliss unbroken intense!

(Translation, author's)

It is as the Katha Upanishad describes. "The sun doesn't shine there, nor the moon and the stars, not the lightning even; then how much such fire? It is only after that light shines do these shine. It is the light which illumines all the world." As the Bible claims: "Let there be light and there was light." Describing this light S.K. Ghosh claims that when Shrivas saw him (Nimai): "He saw a human form covered with, as it seemed to him a dazzling light, or rather a light which ought to have dazzled but didn't." When Lord Krishna entered into Nimai's body at the house of Shrivas in his worship room the devotees had the same experience as described by 'clinically dead person's had seen. They claim that these persons saw "a body appearing to them to be consisting of strong light only, and not of flesh and blood. That light, though brighter than that of the mid-day sun, was quite serene, and agreeable to behold. It soothed and delighted but did not dazzle."

Apart from the vision so professed with an unearthly light the other characteristics of Nimai's swoon or trances in which Sri Krishna is related to have manifested in him, was that he was unaware of them all the time. It would all happen during his period of unconsciousness during which he would lie as one dead, often devoid even of breath. Later his followers and companions would have a hard time viewing him. At times they would even despair for their life. Mr. Ghosh describes one happening in the following way, when Nimai's happened to be at Shrivas's house. "After much care he (Nimai) was restored to consciousness. One regaining his consciousness he looked around at those who were near him. "Is not this your house, Pundit' said Nimai addressing Shrivas. "Yes I know it is your house, but how come I to be here?" After a little reflection he continued. "I feel as if I had been dreaming! And did I rave?" They explained to him that he had a fainting fit, but had not raved at all.

At times Vishwambhara (Nimai) himself explained these mystical incidents in which he actually become Krishna thus to Shrivas when he wanted to convince him (Nimai) that he did show himself in the form of Shri Krishna to his friend called Nityananda. Nimai said: "Did I? If that be the case, I cannot tell you how it came about. I am utterly helpless at such times, and if any wonder happens through me I have his knowledge how it comes to pass. I assure you I have no control over these extra-ordinary events. If they happen at all, they come or go of their own accord. Also according to the accounts available to us, Nimai had given them the power of initiations by mere touch as Sri Ramkrishna Paramhansa exercised in converting the agnostic Narendra – the real name of Swami Vivekananda. This way Nimai also made many of his companions receive the boon of devotion. Shuklambar, Nimai's neighbour and a revered ascetic, for example, asked him to grant him the divine bhakti of Shri Krishna. In the celebrated Chaitanya Bhagwat it is mentioned that Nimai lifted his hands and said: 'Be blessed'! "Then it is described that no sooner did the Lord (Nimai) say this than a thrill passed through his frame, his hair stood on end, and tears rolled down his checks. He felt himself overpowered by a shine of celestial ecstasy, and relived of all the impurity of his soul; and presently with his mendicant-bag thrown across his shoulder he began to dance like a man drunk with joy."

This drastic change in Nimai's personality was very joyfully received by the Vaishavites of Navadweep. It was quite astounding to see a prankist and pedantic Nimai turning into a serene devotee. Advaita, a Sanskrit scholar told all of them that Krishna had appeared in a dream to him. It is said that he had some doubt about the interpretation of one of the Shlokas of the Geeta. When Advait slept he dreamt some one was calling him and he heard a voice saying: "Don't worry! I have myself come in answer to your prayer. I have come for salvation of humanity." Then he saw it was Nimai and felt as if he was saying all this to confirm his manifesting Lord Krishna's form. Still Advait doubted, misled by Nimai's humility and his prostrating himself before him. Advait thought that if he was Shree Krishna, why would be lie prostrate before him this way. It was much later Advait was finally converted when he was called by Nimai through Ramai. It is claimed by the biographers of Nimai that when Advait entered Shrivas's room where Nimai was present he saw nothing but: "a form brighter than a thousand moons; and fairer far than a thousand gods of love. "He also saw numerous celestial beings offering prayers to the Lord, for at Shrivas's house shree Krishna's divine spirit had entered Nimai.

By this time Nimai had become almost the leader of the local Vaishnavites. When the Vaishnavas told him they were being persecuted he became very angry and began to shout in rage. "I will teach them a lesson for I am no other than Shree Krishna."

Seeing Nimai's condition, however, Shachi was somewhat nervous for her son's behaviour resembled with that of a mad person. In desperation she summoned Shrivas to help her. Coincidentally when Shrivas went near Nimai and the latter rose to salute him he was overcome by emotion and fell into a swoon. Shrivas recognised it as a symptom of the deepest devotions and reassured Shachi that it wasn't at all any madness or disease.

I was about this time that at the joint initiative of Advait and Nimai that the Vaishnavas now started their kiratan (or as it is popularly called, Sankirtan) at latter's house. Narhari Sarkar Thakur has described this beginning of the Sankirtan in his "Since Krishna Bhajanamritam" the following way:

"Clad only in a loin cloth he drowned with his bliss in the ocean of love for all kinds of beings – the monist unbelievers, men blinded by wealth, sham yogis, dullards, drunkards, sinners, out castes, yavanas(muslims) fools and ignorant women and made them feel as though they were in heaven. He cleansed their minds of evil. He induced the men to dance with the delicacy and grace of women so that like the milkmaids of Vraja, their thoughts went out to Shri Krishna."

The biographers of Chaitanya Mahaprabhu as Nimai eventually came to be known – claim that Shankirtana perhaps started in the summer of 1509. Shachi asked Galadhar to be always with her son lest he come to any harm. Meanwhile rumours were afloat that the Muslim monarch did not like this new development and might take action against the noisy vaishnavas. Shrinivas was particularly afraid. Nimai came to know of it and to reassure him appeared one day at his house in the form of four-armed Vishnu with couch, discus, club and lotus. Shrivas was wonder-struck and started reading verses from the Bhagwat Purana in his praise. His family also had the vision of the lord and they worshipped him with flowers they had bought for the Vishnu-pooja. Nimai told Shrivas not to be afraid of the Sultan or his soldiers. He then went away charging him not to tell the incident to any one.

It was about this time Nityanand came to Navadweepa. He was to become a close friend of Nimai and was to be called Nitai. Nityananda had been travelling for twenty years, visiting numerous pilgrimage spots. At Vrindavan he had met Iswar Puri. Hearing from him about the advent of Nimai, he hastened to Nadia. Nimai went out to meet the ascetic himself accompanied by some of his companions. He took Nityananda to the house of Shrivas, where the Vaishnavas used to gather. He first showed himself as an incarnation of Balrama. Nimai then disclosed to him the form of Shri Gauranga with six arms, two with bow and arrows, one with a flute and the last two with danda and kamandal(staff and water bowl). Nitai(as Nimai began to address Nityananda out of affection) fell into a trance. When he swooned he broke his staff and threw away the water pot he earned by virture of being an 'avadhoota sannyasi'. Nimai took him to Shachi and told her, he was like a brother to him and she should look upon him as Vishwarupa (Nimai's lost elder brother). Indeed Nitai resembled Shachi's Elder son who was no more. "Chaitanya-Mangala" records Shachi's happiness in the following way :

> "She felt a mother's love for Nitai.
> Her voice was choked with emotion, tears flowed.
> Her heart was gladdened as she saw before her.
> Her sons, and all her sorrow vanquished."

It was around middle of that year (1509) that Nimai become the acknowledged leader of the Nawadweep Vaishnavas. This sect later came to be known as 'Gaudia-vaishnavas' or the 'Chaitanya Sampradaya'. Barring Advait all had become part of this group. It was strange that Advait who very earnestly prayed Lord Krishna to incarnate was the last to join this group. Now the Sankirtan(group singing accomplanied by dance, playing upon the musical instrument and dancing) had regualrly began at the courtyard of Shrivas. There is, however, and interesting episode attacthed with Advait's joining the group. It was his desire that Nimai should place his feet upon his head. When Advait along with his wife came to Shrivas's place Nimai told him – "It was your prayer which brought me out of the milk of ocean I had him lying in. Your prayers and loud cries induced me to come down to earth to end human misery. In fact all devotees have taken birth because of you". Whereupon Advait performed the ritual worship and his desire was fulfilled when Nimai placed his foot upon his lead. When Advait was asked to seek a boon he didn't demand anything for his person but prayed that in this sect every one should be admitted irrespective of caste and sex considerations or even qualification of any education. Nimai gladly agreed and then this Chaitanya sect became renowned for its catholicity.

Soon all the Vaishnavas started gathering for Sankirtan every night either at Shrivas's place or that of other devotee Chandrashekhar. In these Sankirtans Nimai(Vishshambhar) openly proclaimed himself as an incarnation : "In the Kali-age I am Narayana. I am the son of Devaki, lord of universe."

"One day he asked them to sing his Abhishek Geeta (Coronation-song), a kind of glorification to the Lord. On this day he revealed himself at Shrivas's house. Sitting on the raised seat meant for the worship of Vishnu he asked the devotees to sing hymns. Gadadhar put flowers garlands around his neck, Nityananda held an umbrella over him and Narahari waved a Chamar (whisk). Suddenly the persons standing around Nimai saw his body glowing with an effulgence beyond compare. Then they offered him clothes, garlands, food, fruits and many other things, and he gladly accepted them all, vindicating the lord's commitment in Bhagwat-Gita:"A leaf, a flower, a fruit or water offered to me by a devotee with pure heart that offering I partake of (by appearing in human form)." Lord Krishna appearing through Nimai disappointed no one by partaking all that was offered as Prasad. It is said in a short time he ate food suffcient to have fully fed as many as hundreds of persons. One of the biographers of Chaitanya Mahaprabhu in Bengali says that even Nimai's mother, Shachi was also among the persons who paid homage to Lord Krishna appearing through Nimai's form. In fact she was the one who performed the 'Aarti'(circumambulating lighted lamps kept in a huge plate round the deity's idol or image or visage). The biographer says that though Shachi knew no Sanskrit, while performing the Aarti she also recited a Shloka from Srimadbhagwat which contains a prayer of Devaki to the new-born Krishna. Although this is said to be a miracle yet it could be just that hearing the prayer she had memorised it. Shridahar who had scoffed at Nimai for the later's declaring he was 'Father of Ganga', now hastened to make amends. He was offered a boon to repay you all the things I took from you by force' as Nimai told him. He was offered lordship of an empire, but that was refused too. When Nimai insisted Shridhar said: "Then grant me this: let the young and beautiful brahmin who snatched away all my things like plantain leaves etc., also take possession of my heart and make his permanent abode there." "So also Haridas asked the boon that the Lord might make him the abject servant of all thy servants."

Incidentally, Haridas was a Muslim who belonged to Buran in the sub-division of Jessore. Later on he adopted Hinduism and became ardent devotee of Lord Krishna. He used to chant aloud the name of 'Hari' to the great chagrin of the Muslim quazi. But despite the stern warming Haridas did'nt cease to chant aloud 'Hari'. Ultimatly he, Haridas, refused to recant, the quazi got him whipped at each of the twenty turnings of the market. But according to Chaitanya-Bhagwat' Haridas declared that 'even of he were hacked to pieces he won't cease chanting Hari's Name.' But miraculously even while being whipped Haridas felt no pain. Not only that he even prayed god to forgive his tormentors. It is said that while chanting 'Hari's' name Haridas went in to trance even when whipped. Deeming him to be dead the tormentors threw him in the shallow part of the river. But soon revived, Haridas came back and an astounded Quazi fell at his feet and asked forgiveness.

But when the Abhishek-Geetā was sung with due ceremony Nimai(as Lord Krishna) declared that when the lashes had fallen on Haridas he had taken him on his bosom so that they might not hurt Haridas's back where they eventually fell. At the Abhisheka ceremony many devotees came to have a glimpse of Nimai and received benediction of the Lord conveyed by him. One of the biographers (S.K. Das) describes the scene the following way:

"......they (the people assembled at Shrivas' house) came to realise the situation, and they saw that the material world had almost disappeared from their eyes. Their eyes were riveted on the Lord (Nimai as Krishna). He was on the dais. He was no doubt Nimai, but his body seemed to be made of electricity, of a yellowish-shine light which though more brilliant than the rays of the mid-day sun, did not hurt the eyes in the least, but so soothed and pleased them that it was ecstasy in itself to behold it. They further saw that the light was emitted not only from the person of the lord, but from every one present there. Indeed it was seen that light was being emitted from every substance there, the stools, the utensils, the clothing; in fact everything was covered and suffered with luminosity, even the atmosphere of the room."

Following the Abhishek ceremony Nimai returned

to his normal form, as usual-after the trance. But he was reportedly surprised to see so many persons around him. He asked : "Well? What is the matter to-day?" His ignorance about all that happened before convinced scholars and learned person that their Nimai was no other than the divine Lord Krishna in person disguised as a human being. May be they were carried away by their own devotion for Lord Krishan and saw Nimai as Lord Krishna personified. But there is no doubt that all those present there did see Nimai as Lord Krishna while Nimai himself was consciously ignorant. As Goswami Tulsidas declares :

Jākee rahee bhāvana jaisee!
Prabhu moorat dekhi tin taisee!

(One beholds one's god according to one's feeling of devotion)

After all the divine element permeates every soul. When some establish direct communication with their chosen Lord they in the process enhance their divinity level which to an outside viewer appears like a celestial halo. Nimai's communication with Lord Krishna is without doubt – not only because people saw it but because what he himself felt. Goswami Tulsidas further says :

Tehi jānahu jehi deu janaayee!
Jaanat tumhhi tumahi hui jāyee!!

(Only he knows you whom you want to be known. And once he knows you he becomes you yourself)

So where and how god manifests Himself depends upon His sweet will. But it is the purity of emotion that brings one near God. The Hindu belief holds that body is a veil over soul which is instinct with divinity. It is the purity of soul which makes heart blemishless and hence body a veil transparent. Nimai's soul had achieved that purity to make his chosen Lord reveal Himself through him only.

V. The Sankirtan Triumphs

We have already referred that Nimai or Vishshambhar had initiated the process of Sankirtan at a very meagre scale. Although this Sankirtan was very much part of the society it was generally individualised. Normally few persons used to gather earlier for this in one individual's house. But after the revelation of Krishna in him he started intensifying it. In fact after Vishambhara's states became longer and longer in duration other people around him used to sing Krishna's name to revive him. Vishambhar now decided to spread the practice of Sankirtan so as to make it more universal. Thus far those only close to him who formed the inner circle would take part in sankirtan and that too at an individual's house behind closed doors. For popularising it Nimai choose Nitai and Haridas who visited every house to exhort people to join the sankirtan in large number.

Like in every society Nawadweep's also had some people who were rogue by nature. They would while away their time drinking and loitering and were against any noble work. When Nitai and Haridas visited two of such persons, known goondas, Jagai and Madhai, they hit them with heavy objects as much as to drench them with blood. When Vishambhara came to know about it and saw blood on Nitai's head, he rushed to the spot where they two ruffians had assaulted him, but was prevented from doing anything rash by Nitai, who praised Jagai for having restrained his companion from hitting him a second time. Nimai, in his gratitude embraced Jagai who fainted at his touch. On coming to senses, in stead of Nimai's he saw the four-armed Vishnu holding conch discus, club and lotus in his hands. He fell into a swoon. Vishambhara revived him by placing his foot upon his breast. Madhai was also resentful and at Nimai's bidding sought Nityananda's (Nitai's) forgiveness. Then the two reformed goons fell at Nimai's feet. Not only that they recited a long verse in his praise which surprised all the devotees present. Nimai then consoled them by saying that he had taken upon himself - the sins committed by those two ruffians.

This incident did cast a great effect on the people of Navadweepa or Nadia. Now they were getting increasingly convinced that Nimai had some super human powers. What was more, on Nimai's exhortation Madhai, who wanted to do something to expatiate his sins built a bathing ghat on the Gangā river. Thenceforward he remained a celibate staying on that ghat only.

Writing about the subsequent events Nimai's biographers claim that at this very time Advaita criticised Nimai for living like a prince and self glorifying him. This scathing comment made Nimai so depressed and hurt that he tried to jump into the Gangā to end his life. However, Nityananda and Haridas were watchful enough to bring him back to safety. Nimai then hid himself at the house of Nandan Acharya. Advaita felt so remorseful that he began to fast. Hearing about that Nimai what to Acharya's place and found him almost fainting because of weakness. He reassured Advaita, and Acharya begged him to confer on him Dāsya bhāva (devotion of slave-master relationship). Nimai readily did so. At Nimai's suggestion it was decided thereafter to stage Krishan Leela (mortal acts of Lord Krishna's divine performance as a human being). Curiously enough Buddhi manta Khan got the costumes, and the play was enacted at Shrivas's house. Nimai played the role of Rukmini and then as Jagat Janani (mother of the cosmos). He acted so well that audience and the actors both felt so enraptured that they recited verses in the goddess's praise "and sucked the breast of Nimai in devotional ecstasy".

Despite recognising presence of the diving spark in

Nimai's person the problem with Nimai's old friend was that Nimai never treated them as unequal. One of them was Advait who wanted Nimai to treat him not as a savant but as a servant. In order to instigate Nimai Advaita had the rumour floated through a reliable source that he had forsaken the path of devotion and embraced the path of monism which deemed knowledge to be supreme. Hearing this Nimai came charging at him and dragging Advait from his seat threw him on the ground while beating him madly. "If you had to forsake the path of devotion why did you make me leave my abode in the milky ocean and come to these mortal please?" Advaita wanted this only. Achieving his objective he fell at Nimai's feet and begged him to treat him (Advaita) as his servant. Vishambhara (Nimai) recovered from his rage and realising the truth embraced Advaita with the grant of this wish. Then all present there wept feelingully.

It was about time Nimai began to popularise worship through Sankirtan. The holy chant, popular till to-day, given below was first popularised by Nimai only:

"Hare Krishna Hare Krishna, Krishna Krishna Hare Hare
Hare Rām Hare Rām Rām Rām Hare Hare."

This chant grew so much in popularity and its widening acceptance all over the Vaishnava cult all over the world that now we have a full institution devoted to Sankirtan, after being sung in selected gatherings, spilled into the streets with Nimai leading a large number of people, all swinging and dancing and playing music. Since it made no restriction on any basis whatever it spread like a jungle fire all over. Sankirtan is simple, devoid of any pre requisites except feeling of an intense longing for being one with the Deity.

This religious community singings caught the people's imagination. But they appeared as an eye-sore to the Muslim Quazi. According to some accounts it was a section of the Hindus themselves which out of jealousy to Nimai's uncontrollably waxing popularity instigated the Muslim Quazi. But it seems more likely that the Quazi himself began to fear it as a precessor of some kind of insurrection. Moreover, as it was, being a Muslim he wouldn't have at all liked such noisy and large scale demonstration of the infidel's faith. So he and his soldiers began to patrol the streets. They did beat up some of the singers, break up their drums and instilled terror in their minds.

In fact this disturbance had occurred due to some high caste Hindus not taking kindly to the admission of the low caste people in the Kirtan Mandalis (assemblies for group singing) and their instigating the Quazi. Besides the name of God, they reasoned, such processions ought to be taken out silently and not by shouting and singing. When Nimai heard of it he was filled with rage and decided to defy the oppressive Quazi. At once he called Nitai to make the announcement that very evening a large kirtan process would be taken out. Now he was so annoyed that he decided to teach the Quazi a bitter lesson. Nimai's this declaration was received joyfully by the local Vaishnavas and their fears dwindled. And when the Master, himself the embodiment of Lord Krishna, led the procession from the front, who could have stopped it?

The huge Kirtan party was split into four groups, led each by Advaita, Haridas, Shrivas and the fourth group by no other than Nimai and Nitai. It was truly a memorable receiving and all the residents of Nadia enthusiastically joined it. Indeed the concourse was so mammoth that some people wondered whether the divine beings had not descended to the mortal world to behold the ceremony. Often falling into a swoon, Nimai, especially decked for the occasion looked every inch a divine being himself. Describing the occasion, S. K. Ghos writes: "The dancing figure of the lord was like the full moon distributing gladness all round him. The lord then no longer looked like a being of this world. The vast crowd saw that a holy light was being emitted by his head. The lord was dancing with uplifted arms and his gaze directed upward, while the following song was being sung: "Let my heart cling to thy feet, O My Krishna.

With the tempo of the Kirtan gaining momentum every second of it, more and more people were drawn to it. Their enthusiasm knew no limit. Mr. Ghosh continues: "Strangers embraced one another as though they were old dear friends. Some sat down and besmeared themselves with dust, as if it was the most pleasant occupation in the world. Others sat and wept, and wept uncontrollably. Some took it into their hands the dust taken from the feet of anyone that happened to come across and thus pleased themselves and Shri Krishna with their humility. Some danced with uplifted hands totally forgetting of the presence of others. Some found themselves impelled by excessive devotion to prostrate themselves before everyone they found before themselves."

"There were many who appeared to have become stark mad. Some of them ascended the trees and thence jumped to the ground, indifferent to the risk of their limbs.

It appeared as a huge python drunk in the Bhakti was gradually crawling towards the Quazi's house. Nimai was in an unforgiving and militant mood and instead his usual 'Haribol!' he sang: "My mind is at thy feet, O wielder of the bow" and he danced with the name of Shiva on his lips - as though verily dancing the eerie Tanndav Dance."

The frenzy was such that the mob surrounded the Quazi's house and destroyed everything if could lay its hands on. The Quazi, greatly pulverised, fled with his family and retinue and subordinates. Indeed had people with a cool head not intervened the Quazi's house would have been burnt down to ashes - for the people were so frenzically charged by Nimai's exhortation. Although earlier the Quazi did try to intercept the procession but his consulates and sepoy appeared drowned in that sea of humanity. It is said that one old man who was sent by the Quazi reported that as he went lightning fell closely and singed his white beard - an unmistakable sign of the divine wrath.

When Nimai's rage subsided he sent for the Quazi with the promise that he would not be harmed. The Quazi then came and bowed respectfully, appeared to have been overawed by Nimai's divine presence and the large following Nimai then asked him as to why he had hid himself when the former came to house as the guest? The visibly shaken Quazi replied that since Nimai appeared to be in a wrathful mood he thought better to hide himself and save his life, adding that: "I used to call your grandfather uncle, so in a way you are my nephew". Thus the Quazi made up with Vishambhara. Indeed the circumstances in which he found himself he could have no other alternative.

Then Vishambhara (Nimai) made the Quazi promise that he would never interfere with the Sankirtana.

This way the matter was amicably settled and the Kirtana singers continued with their song and dance. The Quazi wished to follow them for some distance, but Nimai instructed him not to do so. And then the Sankirtan registered his final triumph.

Sankirtan is so closely associated with Nimai's personality as non violence is with Gandhi or love with Christ. His this unique gift to Hinduism is still gaining in popularity. It is because Sankirtan is essentially a collective ceremony. People feel bound with a thread of devotional unity. No wonder it gained pace in the democratic world as much as to be vibrating the firmaments of right from Los Angeles to Brisbane nowadays.

so in a way you are my nephew." Thus the Quazi made up with Vishambhara. Indeed the circumstances in which he found himself he could have no other alternative.

Then Vishambhara (Nimai) made the Quazi promise that he would never interfere with the Sankirtana.

This way the matter was amicably settled and the Kirtana singers continued with their song and dance. The Quazi wished to follow them for some distance, but Nimai instructed him not to do so. And then the Sankirtan registered this final triumph.

Sankirtan is so closely associated with Nimai's personality as non violence is with Gandhi or love with Christ. This is the unique gift to the world, is still gaining in popularity. It is because Sankirtan is essentially a collective ceremony. People feel bound with a thread of devotional unity. No wonder it gained base in the democratic world as much as it is becoming the armamentarius of right from Los Angeles to Brisbane in Australia.

VI. Renouncing the Family Life

Following the Quazi episode Nimai stayed at Nawadweepa some months more. But now gradually he had started feeling the urge to renounce the family bondage and go in the guest of his Krishna who ever appeared so close yet still quite far. Now Krishna's presence was felt by Nimai increasingly and for longer periods. It was then that an incident occurred which expedited his migration to asceticism, renouncing the familial world.

One day he was sitting on the bank of the holy river Gangā, deeply engrossed in his thought and absent - mindedly chanting 'Gopi-Gopi', mentally experiencing the Gopies love for Krishna. All of a sudden a student came there and said: "Better you repeat the name of Krishna for chanting 'Gopi-Gopi' won't take you anywhere." Feeling disturbed and peeved somewhat at such interruption in his reverie Nimai lost his temper and grabbing a stick lying closeby he rushed to beat that boy. The student ran away and denounced this act among his fellow students. Since the boy happened to be a brahmin his all friends became angry and decided to teach Niami a bitter lesson so that he might never dare insult a brahmin. But before they could contemplate doing so Vishambhar realised that he won't get people's respect if he continued to be a family man. So he set his mind on taking Sannyas.

It was about this time a monk called Krishna Bhārti came to Nadia. He agreed to initiate Vishambhara, Nityananda Mukund, Gadadhar and a few other. Shachi was also apprised of Nimai's this decision. The local Vaishnavas who learnt about Nimai's embracing asceticism tried their best to dissuade him. But Nimai was firm. His this decision made her mother weep and almost swoon in sorrow. According to his biographer he consoled her saying.

"You were my mother in all my previous incarnations. When you were Prishni, I was born to you as your son; then you were successfully born as Aditi, Devhuti, Kaushalya and Devaki, and I was born as you son, Vamana, Kapila, Ramchandra and Krishna. I promise you that I shall be born as your son in two more births. So please do not grieve for me."

With these consoling words he further strengthened his resolve then he continued spending his time in sankirtan, Soon the appointed night came when he decided to go to Katva to be initiated in to monastic life. His mother wept for whole night. The vaishnavas had already left. Haridas and Gadadhar remained with him. They wanted to go with him but he stopped them. Finally Nityananda, Mukund went with him till Katva. Comforting his mother again, he acknowledged his debt to her with gratitude, and said:

"Mother, you have brought me up; you have educated me. You always looked after my comfort, not for a moment have you thought for yours. What you have done for me I shall not be able to repay even after a millions births; for ever I shall remain indebted to you. Mother, it is God's will, no one has the power to be really independent, it is he who brings together and then separates us; who can fathom his will........"

Katva was a village twenty four miles away from Nadia. It was here that Vishambhara was initiated by his guru Keshava Bharti who said: "I realise that you are a divine being and the jagat guru (the preceptor of the world). Still I am initiating you for the form's sake.

With guru's permission Vishambhara got his head shaved and them bathed in the Ganga. As he emerged from the river after his prayers, Keshava Bharti gave him the name SHREE KRISHNA CHIATANYA (literally meaning he who awakens Shri Krishna in the hearts of others). Hence forward, in this book also he would be referred as Chaitanya or Chaitanya Mahaprabhu. Now he became a monk, a free man from the filial bondage.

So we have seen how a naughty prankster turned into a somber ascetic. This transformation, however, was not swift. But what remained unchanged in him was the transparency of the heart. What made him a divine person was his this essential characteristic. No matter where it burns the light must cast its radiance. This transformation can be classified into many stages: a gay cavalier prankster, a somewhat sobre teacher, the pioneer in starting the cult of worship through Kirtan and finally a Sannyasi. Some of the old accounts claim that certain student recalcitrant behaviour expedited Nimai's transformation to Chaitanya. But it must be understood that people like Nimai never renounce the world out of fear. They do so when their inner urge goads them to their ultimate destination. The animosity of a handful students could hardly have been instrumental either in his departure from Nadia or in his taking up the monastic life. In fact it was his inner urge which forced him to become a monk and spread Vaishnavism far and wide. Moreover, when one detects the divine spark in his soul, no worldily bond can ever bind them. Who would long for tap water if one has the Gangā at his door? Who would care for stars when one beholds the rising sun? When one has one's soul illumined by a divine light can anything spreading mortal darkness stop it? Could Gautam Buddha been stopped by the lure of wealth and the pleasure of senses? Could Shakaracharya be stopped by his mother's affection? It seems Chaitanya wished to spread Vaishnavism as Shankaracharya did who snapped all fetters to spread his teachings of Advaitism. These personages are mini-incarnations of the supreme being who grace the world to accomplish twin objective: raise themselves to the highest state of spiritualism and then to redeem others. God had proclaimed in the Srimadbhagwat Geetā that he continues to descend to the mortal plane for eliminating vices and enhancing virtues. The Gita says God takes a human shape with all the inherent frailties of man through his Yogamaya (illusive creation) for the world's redemption. Chaitanya came to instinct the people with Bhakti. It may be mentioned that at the time of his advent the social and political conditions of Bengal were appalling. Writing about them Jayananda in

'Chaitanya Mangal' says: "He (the foreigner ruling there) would ask his sepoys to break the sacred threads of priests; he would spit in their mouths so that they ventured not to fetch cowdung to plaster their house. "It was during Hussain Shah's (1481-88) reign that Chaitanya was born. The Shah persecuted his Hindu subjects particularly the brahmins of Navadweep. He is said to have destroyed the images of the Jagannath temple as stated in 'Madala Panji". Chaitanya's biographies also record the destruction of many temples at Muslim king's hands.

The period of Chaitanya was marked with the rise of mysticism and asceticism on one hand while on the other hand rise of the revolting practices coming increasingly in vogue. The atmosphere was often unspiritual and the people were skeptical about the efficacy of devotion. It was due to the domination by the foreigner's rule. The Muslims rulers were generally occupying the throne of authority all over the country and by that time they had not adopted India as their own country. They still considered it an alien country teeming with infidels whom they had by their moral and spiritual duty, to curb and bring into total submission. In fact this Medieval Age was marked by the rise of Bhakti all over the land. When the mortal authority brings no satisfaction to the people their seeking the protection of God is a natural consequence. The advents of Kabir, Tulsi, Surdās, etc. in the north also signify this sense of resignation among the masses. People were in general, reduced to acute penury because the alien rulers had usurped all the wealth of the country. This left the countrymen with no alternative whatever than to worship God, in the simplest way possible, to come to their rescue. Hence pure Bhakti Marg appealed to such distressed people quite naturally. And the devotees like Chaitanya showed them the way. They proved how one could be close to God even when almost a pauper. The main emphasis of this age was on simplicity, shorn of all affectations. It was in this very period that Kabir proclaimed:

"Kabir, why, O Mullah,

Climbest thou upto thy minaret?

Thinkest thou that the Lord is hard of hearing?

Seek in thy heart for Him for whose sake

Thou so loudly callest to prayer?

It was these conditions that made Advaita, the head of the Vaishnava sect pray to God on the bank of river Bhagirathi river to send his incarnation on Earth: "Father

Shri Krishna! My Lord and beloved protector! The misery of mankind pains me. I know the cause of this misery is their own wickedness. They have forgotten the Fatherhood of god and the brotherhood of man and are seriously quarreling from motives of selfishness as dogs do over a piece of bone."

[As mentioned in S.K. Ghose's "Gaurang, Or Salvation of All"]

VII. Wanderings of A Monk

Chaitanya's desire was to go to Vrindavan forthwith his initiation ceremony at Katva. So he immediately set out to reach there but he continued to roam for three days and night, lost in his love for Krishna. He eventually managed to reach as far as Radha in Burdwan district. Nityananda, who had no idea where they had reached, pretended that the way to Vrindavan was right opposite to the one they had taken. Thus he managed to dissuade Chaitanya from further travelling as Chaitanya had travelled without food or rest. But when Chaitanya insisted to see the river Yamuna Nityananda pointed out to the river Gangā and claimed that it was that. Of course this was pure falsehood but it was spoken with noble intention. Hence not a sin. In the meanwhile Advaita managed to pursue Chaitanya to rest at his house. In the evening they again indulged in their Sankirtan and sang: "Inaffable is my joy as Krishna has at last come to my house." They continued to dance for three hours after which Chaitanya was persuaded to rest. The following morning the news travelled far and wide about Chaitanya's reaching there which made a crowd of people swell around the house they were staying. Knowing about his son's whereabouts Shachi, Chaitanya's mother, also came there since the place not far off from Nadia. Though she again mildly persuaded Chaitanya to return home, realising Chaitanya couldn't do so without breaking the monastic rule so she suggested that Chaitanya should stay put at Nilanchala (as Puri was known that time). Puri wasn't far away from Nadia and the contact could easily be maintained.

Although Shachi could reconcile to her son's embracing monastic order, Chaitanya's wife, Vishnupriya, found it difficult to bear. It was obvious for a young wife, hardly fifteen years old. She had also requested Chaitanya the following way: "Don't desert me, my lord! I cannot live without you. Do not forsake your innocent wife." Chaitanya was at his wits' end, so he sought divine help. And low and behold, Chaitanya appeared to her in the form of Vishnu, the Lord of lords. But Vishnupriya was not confounded. She fell down at the Lord's feet and asked from him the boon of keeping her husband as he was (i.e. in human form). Lord Vishnu was bound by the boon so couldn't refuse her. However, it was Chaitanya who gradually brought her round to accepting the inevitable with the promise: "I give my commitment to you, as I have promised to my mother, that whenever you feel an ardent desire to see me, I will come and soothe you, and you will see me in your heart."

Before departing finally Chaitanya gave his wife an affectionate farewell. She appeared before him dressed beautifully, looking every inch a queen and they passed the night together – the last – in the conjugal delight. This was before Chaitanya took the vow of Sanyas. Then after he departed leaving her soundly asleep.

Meanwhile Chaitanya's departure from Nadia made the place quite mournful. "The images of the gods' "as a poet said," in the temple of Nadia look pale and devoid their charms." The shops were closed. Shrivas, at whose house Nimai's Kirtan assemblies were held could not forget him whether conscious or unconscious. Often when gathering flowers for worship his mind longed for those days when their beloved was with him. He would wistfully look at the silent court yard which once resounded with the holy chant of Hari and the twinkling of anklets, the twang of the drum and the jingle of Kartal (cymbals), and tear would well up in his eyes. He felt almost as the Gopis did when Krishna departed for Mathura. Vishnupriya could hardly eat anything for the excessive sorrow she felt.

Nimai's mother Shachi fasted non stop for 12 days and became exceedingly weak. Once she dreamt her son appeared and said: "Mother I have traveled to many places as a sanyasi but nowhere could I stay without seeing you," the dream comforted her somewhat.

At that time there was great bitterness between Raja Prataprudra and Hussain Shah, the respective rulers of Orissa and the Gaur emperor in whose domain (Gaur) fell Nadia. But seeing Chaitanya determined to cross in Orissa despite the hurdles, an official of the Shah, Ramchandra Khan, came to the great devotee's (Chaitanya's) help. At last Chaitanya stepped into Orissa. As Chaitanya and his companions did so they first bowed to pay their homage to the land of their birth.

They reached Remuna after a short journey from where they went to Cuttack, renowned for temple of Sakshee-Gopal. From Cuttack they went to Bhuvneshwara and bathed in the Vindu Sarovar and went to the Lingaraja Temple where Chaitanya danced in front of the image of Shiva.

After staying for the night in Bhuvneshwara, they proceeded onwards. Chaitanya bathed in the river Bhargi (also called Bhargovi) which was six miles north of Puri. There he handed over his staff to Nityananda and went off to worship in the Shiva Temple. Perhaps not digesting Chaitanya's showing his devotion to Lord Shiv, Nityananda or Nitai was not happy, so he broke Chaitanya's stick (staff) into three pieces. Though Chaitanya was annoyed his annoyance took entirely different shape. When he heard what happened, he forbade his companions to enter Puri with him and thus containing them to walk some distance behind him.

Chaitanya was thrilled to see the tall spire of the Jagannath temple and began to dance in the excessive joy. He rushed to the temple imagining that Krishna was calling him and madly responding with the exclamations: "I come! I come!"

The image in the temple was an extra ordinary one. It was seated on a throne in the Garbha-Griha (sanctum samctorum) of the temple. It was bathed, fed (simulated to give the impression of its eating) and at night laid on the bed. It was fanned in summer and covered with a quilt in a cold winter. There were innumerable servants employed to look after it, of which the most prominent was the king Prataprudra himself. The king would sweep the passage leading to the temple with a broom of gold! The image was guarded day and night by the sentries. Everyone couldn't just enter the temple without any check. So when

Chaitanya rushed to the inner apartments quick as a flash of lightning the sentries were caught unawares. To their consternation Chaitanya jumped on the platform and clasped the huge idol to his bosom. Then he fell down before it in a swoon. The guards rushed forth to the assault the lad that had dared enter thus and raised their sticks to beat him. But a tall elderly majestic brahmin stepped forth and covering Chaitanya with his protective hands, cried: "Stop ye fool! Don't you see him a holy man, if not God himself!" The man who thus intervened was no other than Vasudeva Sarvabhauma, in religious hierarchy of the temple second only to the king Prataprudra himself. Vasudeva held a piece of fine cotton at the unconscious ascetic's nose. It stirred. This, he realised was a sign of the Sattvika form of passion for Lord Krishan and was attainable by the devotee who had crossed the highest state of bliss. In the meantime Chaitanya's companions also reached near and were informed that Chaitanya had been taken by Sarvabhauma to his house. Luckily his brother-in-law Gopinath knew Mukunda, Chaitanya's of Nilambar Chakrovarti. Besides Sarvabhuma's father was a class-mate of Nilambar Chakravarti, Chaitanya's maternal grand-father.

Sarvabhauma wanted to teach Chaitanya about Advaitism whereas Gopinath opposed it. This led to a dispute between Gopinath on one side and Sarvabhauma and his disciples on the other. Gopinath claimed Chiatanya to be an incarnation of Shri Krishna. Sarvabhauma quoted the scriptures to refute this. At last Gopinath was exasperated and said the argument was futile since Sarvabhauma would realise it only when the divine grace descended on him. Quoting the Bhagwata he said: "I bow to that omnipotent Supreme God whose power of illusion raises endless controversies among logicians fond of dispute, and keep their souls ever wrapt in delusion." Sarvabhauma proceeded to teach Chaitanya the Vedanta-Sutras. For about a week Chaitanya listened and did not speak a single word. So upset was Sarvabhauma and he asked why Chaitanya had not questioned as a disciple should. Chaitanya replied: "Sir, it is your commentary that was confusing me on the Vedanta-Sutras and not their text. "Then he went on to prove that Brahman was not formless but qualified. Sarvabhauma was awed by Chaitanya's wisdom. Quotating a verse from the Bhagwata, Chaitanya asserted: "Hari bears such attractive qualities that even sages who are free from worldly desires yearn for his devotion." Then on Chaitanya's request Sarvabhauma gave nine interpretations of that shloka. But Chaitanya gave eighteen, each being different and not included in the interpretations given by the renowned servant of Puri. This almost convinced Sarvabhauma that Chaitanya could be no other than Lord Krishna himself as Gopinath had claimed in the beginning. He bowed humbly and sought his grace. Chaitanya appeared to him as the four-armed Vishnu and then as Krishna playing his flute. When Sarvabhauma saw this vision he prostrated himself and then prayed with folded hands. The two embraced each other and danced with joy. Then Chaitanya taught him the following Mantra:

"Harera-nama Harera-nama, Harera-nama aiva kevalam
Kalaun' aasty' eva n'aasty eva n'aaty eva gatir anyatha."

[Except Hari's name indeed there is no salvation in this Kali Age.] Next day Sarvabhauma sent a generous bit from the holy offering of the Jagannath temple and alongwith it a couplet for Chaitanya: "I take refuge in Shri Chaitanya, the ocean of mercy, the incarnation of the one Primieval Man!"

Thus Chaitanya's devotion could convert the great monist of Puri. It gave Chaitanya instant fame for not only Sarvabhauma was considered Puri's leading savant, he was a renowned scholar of that region comprising Bengal, Mithila and Orissa.

The King Prataprudra also didn't have high opinion about ascetics. He abhorred the sight of Sannyasi who would smear dust on his body, weep like a woman. In fact he was really influenced by the Buddhist faith. But when he saw Sarvabhauma vanquished he developed doubt about his own convictions. He did happen to see Chaitanya singing among his companions. The king was quite impressed. He told his one minister" "I never saw such a dance." The king expressed his desire to see Chaitanya. But hearing about it Chaitanya refused point blank, saying that as a Sannyasi he had to remain aloof from the people with power and authority. Prataprudra felt sorry and asked Vasudeva and others to intercede for him. He said that he should not be denied the privilege his common subjects were getting. Eventually the meeting look place when Chaitanya was lying in a swoon in the house of Gopinath and the king went quietly and clasped Chaitanya's feet. But when Chaitanya woke up, he disengaged his feet and said: "Oh! I have touched a man of worldly power." But the king took this remark in his stride and asserted that he was prepared to give up his wealth and power for Chaitanya's sake. This convinced Chaitanya of his sincerity and the two embraced each other. It is said that Prataprudra then also recited some shlokas from Bhagwat. Chaitanya was pleased by the verse which had following: meaning "Highly meritorious must be those persons who extol your nectar-like stories which are not only liferejuvenating to the afflicted but are superior to nectar itself, in-as-much as they are highly eulogised by the knowers of Brahman, and which remove all sins, are most auspicious to hear and the source of all prosperity and are spread all over the world." Chaitanya then also displayed the six-armed form of Lord Vishnu, enjoining him to keep the secret to himself. With the king and the most renowned servant of the monistic faith won over, Chaitanya firmly established Vaishnavism in Orrisa.

Chaitanya's Southward Visit:

Having stayed in Puri for two months he expressed his desire, all of a sudden, to visit South India. Accompanied by a brahmin, Krishnadas, for keeping watch over his belongings while he was in a trance, Chaitanya left Puri going along coast. Chaitanya walked spreadily away singing Krishna's name with the refrain, "save me! Protect me!" Whenever he met a wayfarer he would ask him to chant Hari's name. Thus he made a number of Vaishnava converts. His magnetic personality had a great impact, particularly in the Kanarese and Marathwada. It is mentioned in the accounts that he defeated many scholars on his way such as Ishwar Puri. The Chandipur, Bhargadeva of Tripatra and others. The famous Buddhist leader, Ramgiri, had a debate with him; the Raja of

Trimanda acting as judge. Ramgiri was defeated and became his disciple, adopting the name Haridasa. At a place called Munna he delivered discourses on Krishna and men and women listened with rapt attention and wept with emotion.

Once on his way Chaitanya wandered into the deep forest of Choranandi in which people warmed him, lived a gang of bandits headed by Naoroji. The robbers found him sitting under a tree, and their leader was at once charmed by this lovely young ecstatic. He ordered his man to bring a variety of delicious dishes. But Chaitanya fell into a trance and at waking up at once began to dance. The milk kept there was split and the food scattered while he danced, unmindful. Naoroji was moved with devotion and wept. He threw away all his weapons and asked for the dust of the saints feet. Chaitanya said: "Wear a dress of barks that will be enough and live the life of a mendicant by begging alms. If a handful rice is enough for preserving life what is the use of hoarding money by evil ways? Let the hollow of your palm be your cup, and the fountain be your supply of water. The millionaires, I say, shall have to go to the realms of death. By the same path the emperor and the meanest of his subjects will go." Like the age-old tale concerning the sage Valmiki, Naoroji also repented for his crimes, and putting a dress of bark accompanied

Chaitanya. A few days later, however, be got high fever. Chaitanya tended him himself. Moments after he died. Chaitanya chanted Krishna's name to comfort him. Begging alms from the people he gave him a decent burial.

This way Chaitanya continued to tread on. He drew a large crowd of admirers whenever he went. There were among them ascetics and men and women of high families. All of them wondered at his charming figure and were greatly impressed by his adopting asceticism at such an early age. It is claimed that at times he spoke to them in Tamil and sometimes in Sanskrit. At Gujari he defeated Arjuna, a renowned scholar, in a debate and them stood up and cried aloud: 'Oh, my Krishna!"

It was at this time that he also come in the contact of the harlot called Baramukhi who had great wealth. She observed from her window Chaitanya singing in a maddened state of devotion. She was so moved by the young ascetic that she decided to give up her sinful life and approached Chaitanya with her maid. She opened her long tresses and her beauty was dazzling. She prayed to the saint asking him to save her 'from the bonds of the world! Saying this she cut off her lovely tresses with her own hands. Chaitanya asked her to make a garden of Tulsi plants (basil) and live in chanting Shri Krishna's name.

The harlot handed over everything to her maid, and taking a rosary in her hand began to live, as a Krishna devotee.

When Raja of Travancore heard about Chaitanya be sent a messenger to bring the young ascetic to his palace. On Chaitnaya's refusal to go, he himself went barefooted clad in humble dress to meet the sage. Chaitanya received him with kindness. Another Raja offered many presents which he refused. The Raja begged him to accept alms as he did from others. Chaitanya sent his one disciple Govinda who accepted a handful rice from the Raja's servants.

An account about Chaitanya's doings authored by Krishna-Kaviraya called 'Chaitanya-Charnamrita' narrates many incidents related to Chaitanya's visit to south India. Of course most of them appear imaginary as the poetic style suggests but the most important one is Chaitanya's meeting Ramananda-raya. Although Ramanandaraya was a Shudra (lowcaste person) he was a devout Vaishnava. Sarvabhaum, Chaitanya's old companion, had requested him to meet this fellow definitely. When Chaitanya met him, he also affectionately embraced him. Then followed a long discourse between them about Vaishnava faith. Chaitanya asked him to recite the verse which he thought best expressed it Ramnanda recited the verse after verse, leaving Chaitanya dissatisfied till he finally spoke of the true nature of Radha and Krishna. Given below is the gist of those verses:

1. Faith in Vishnu is got by doing the duties prescribed by one's rank.
2. Resign to Shri Krishna the fruits of your work.
3. The highest means of devotion is to abandon one's caste duties out of love for Krishna.
4. Faith based on knowledge is the highest means of devotion.
5. Faith independent of knowledge is the highest instrument of devotion.
6. Higher than this is Prem-Bhakti (the devotion of love).
7. The lore of servant is higher in the scale of devotion.
8. Love even for a comrade is superior.
9. Love as for a child is higher still.
10. When asked again by Chaitanya what was even higher than that, Ramanandaraya said: "Passion for a love is the highest form of devotion."

Having heard Ramananda speak thus, Chaitanya was overcome with joy an wept. Then Ramananda requested the saint to stay for at least 10 days so that he

[Chaitanya] could reform his sinful heart and confer on him Lord Krishan's love. Chaitanya acceded to this request. In the evening the discourse continued Ramananda said there was no knowledge apart from devotion to Krishna. A devotee is the highest of men and most valuable possession is devotion to Radha and Krishna. Seperation from Krishna was the greatest misery. The devotee should sing song of Radha and Krishna's dalliance and associate with other devotees. He should constantly dwell on the name, qualities and incidents of Krishna's life, live in Vrindavana and sing Krishna's name. The highest meditation is that of Radha and Krishna, their worship is the highest worship and their love songs the sweetest melody. Those who desire mukti (liberation) become like inert bodies. The ill-fated scholar succeeds merely in acquiring dry knowledge while the lucky devotee sips the nectar of Krishna's love. At last Ramanand told Chaitanya that previously he appeared to him as a Sannyasi but now he saw him " a dark complexioned young cowherd enveloped in emanation of a golden coloured deity, revealing the fruit which you hold to your lips and shifting glances of your lotus like eyes. Ramananda guessed that he was Krishna and asked him to reveal himself. Chaitanya then showed him in his true form which none had ever seen before, saying "My complexion is not fair, but it appears fair due to its contacts with the body of Radha who touched none but Krishna." Before leaving he asked Ramananda to retire to Puri who he would him shortly.

While moving about in south Chaitanya also met many Buddhist scholars. They plotted against him and placed before him a plate of unclean rice, saying that it was Vishnu's Prasadam. But, all of a sudden, a huge bird miraculously swooped down and carried of the plate in the beak. The plate then eventually fell on the Buddhist professor's head wounding him and making him unconscious. The Buddhist asked for forgiveness and began to chant Hari's name.

When he reached Srirangam he saw a brahmin devoted to Vishnu, who recited the Gita daily in the temple. Since he (that brahmin) didn't know any Sanskrit he only repeated the verses by rote making many mistakes in the pronunciation. Yet this would affect him, so that he would shed tears, tremble and perspire with devotional fevour. When Chaitanya questioned him he said that when he recited the text he would ever see before him Shri Krishna sitting as Arjuna's Charioteer teaching him the precepts of the holy scriptures. Chaitanya marvelled at his devotion, saying: "You alone are truly worthy to read Gita, as you know the essence of the meaning!"

Going deep south he visited many famous places of pilgrimage including Rameshwaram, Madura Shringiri etc. When he reached Vidyanagar he again met Ramananda who said that since the local king wanted him to reach Puri with lot of manuscripts (some them were given to him by Chaitanya himself) escorted by horsemen etc. it would be better if Chaitanya reached Puri earlier Chaitanya agreed and departed for Puri. As the news of Chaitanya's reached the ears of his disciples and followers a huge concourse of them rushed to welcome their master back home after near two year's roaming about in South India. As he finally reached Puri he immediately went to the Shrine of Puri to pay his respect. Then the whole party dined at Sarvabhauma's house Chaitanya narrated variegated experience of his South Indian travel to his devotees and admirers.

Chaitanya Settles at Puri:

When Chaitanya returned to Puri and the Vaishnavas of Bengal learnt about this it gave them a great joy and they decided to visit Puri.

When the devotees sat around Chaitanya he gazed at them affectionately and asked. "Where is Murari?" Since Murari had fallen in a swoon he was left behind. Then he was called and Chaitanya embraced him. The devotees stayed for four months and thereafter they were persuaded to go back home. Though Nitai, meeting his Nimai after a long gap, did not want to leave the Master (Chaitanya) wanted him to keep on propagating Vaishnavism in Bengal. He exhorted his pet companion of long standing: "Though men in Bengal are quite learned they are not so easily conquered by any display of intellectual powers as by the display of higher emotions. You are all joy; show them what a delight it is to serve Krishna. Appeal to their hearts and show them that there is something else in man besides his intellect. I have the profoundest pity for these learned and intellectual men; kindly take particular care of them." Calling Nitai his dear brother he requested him "to make no exceptions between high and low, wise and ignorant, pious and infidel, good and bad in dispensing your blessings." He said: "the greater the sinner the greater are his claims upon you. Even though you encounter much opposition, overcome it and spread my message."

Although Nitai was unwilling to leave yet entrusted with this responsibility he finally left back home. While Nitai went about spreading Chaitanya's message of love and devotion in Bengal, at Puri Sarvabhaum requested King Prataprudra to allocate a suitable residence for the stay of Chaitanya. The king suggested the house of Kashi Misra near Jagannath temple. He arranged a house which was later known as Gambhira. There, in a small room Chaitanya spent his life at Puri. Chaitanya was happy when Kashi Misra came to welcome him; he embraced Kashi and appeared to him as the four armed Vishnu. Subsequently this house became the centre of activity since many learned scholars and devotees used to flock to see Chaitanya.

Soon the time of the Car Festival (Rath-Yatra) approached closer and Chaitanya expressed his desire to clean the Gundeecha Temple. Kashi Misra, the king's minister ordered for a hundred new pitchers and brooms. Chaitanya rubbed his followers all over with sandal-paste and gave each of them a broom. He began the cleaning campaign by sweeping and cleaning the inside, the roof and the throne. The large and small temples were both washed and swept. Thereafter the dancing hall was taken up. They all chanted Krishna's name for a while, the dust and the dirt were wrapped up in the outer clothing and put aside. It was seen that Chaitanya carried the highest bundle of the dirt and grime. The whole temple was then washed for which a hundred pots full of water were obtained. Thus the temple was made spotlessly clean, Chaitanya himself supervising the work and doing himself a great deal of physical labour. Then the quadrangle of the inner shrine was washed followed by it the cleaning of the whole complex.

Thereafter the Sankirtan took place and Chaitanya with his followers danced with wild delight. Shree Gopal, the son of the Acharya, was so affected by the dance that he fell down into a swoon. All efforts to revive him came to a naught and then Chaitanya laid his hands on the Young lad's breast and cried out : "Rise Gopal!". Lo and Behold, the boy was promptly revived. Thereafter the devotees bathed in the tank and ate of the Mahaprasad (holy offerings). The image of Jagnnath had been tied up and the eyes were repainted as the paint had worn out. 'Chaitanya-Mangal' recaptures the scene the following way: "The image's eyes surpassed the blooming lotus in beauty, his checks flashed radiance like a polished turquoise mirror, his lower tip was more brilliant hued than the 'bandhuli' flower, a light smile spread a ripple of nectar over his form. As the devotees gazed on, the charm of the god's countenance increased every moment, their thirst increased with its gratification; their eyes couldn't move away from that face."

Chariot Festival was to fall the next morning. Chaitanya and his disciples finished their morning rituals early and hastened to the temple. The images of Jagannath (Krishna), Balarama and Subhadra were taken carefully from their thrones and pulled over cotton pillows to the waiting chariots. "Who can move him? The Lord of the universe. He moves of his own will to disport himself?" so claims 'Chaitanya-Charanamrita'. The king Praraprudra himself swept the path with his own hands with a golden broom stick and sprinkled sandal water on the ground. Chaitanya was delighted seeing the king doing all this himself. Amidst the cries of 'Great Lord' the images were finally put in the chariots and the devotees pulled at the ropes. Chaitanya put sandalwood paste on the foreheads of his companions with his own hands and garlanded them all. He divided the kirtana singers into four parties consisting in all twenty four singers and eight men playing on the instruments. Each group had six singers and two persons playing on the mridangas. Prataprudra was watching the dancing and singing with a great delight. He was amazed to see that Chaitanya appeared to be present in every group at the same time. After thus taking part in the Sankirtan Chaitanya selected ten persons from all the groups to join him exclusively in chanting. The remaining devotees encircled them and began to sing. Chaitanya then slowly made his way towards the car of Lord Jagannath and prostrated himself. Then he danced and sang verses in Sanskrit to express his deep salutations to Shri Krishna. Chaitanya's companions thus danced in three circles one outside the other, while the king and his officers formed the outer most circle – a fourth one – a cordon rather then a circle of dancers, to prevent the surging ecstatic crowd from trampling on the dancers who were so immersed in Krishna that they hardly knew what was happening around. Chaitanya also composed a verse of his own addressing it to Lord Jagannath: "I am not one of any of the four castes; nor I am in any of the four Ashramas (householder, forest dweller and wandering medicants). I am slave of him who is the lord of the Gopis; who is the essence of the boundless ocean of nectar and who is universal bliss."

The chariots were now to be escorted on its way to give Darshan to the devotees. Chaitanya went round it and them began to push it with his head. To the wonder of everyone there the heavy chariots began to move just by a push. When the chariot was next stopped on the way it again refused to move notwithstanding even elephants pushing it. Then Chaitanya himself pushed the chariot from behind with his head and lo! It went rattling along. The devotees had just to hold the ropes and it moved on itself. In a moment it reached its final destination. The devotees and the king and all his men were amazed. The images were placed again on their respective thrones and the ceremony of the 'gods' bath and dinner' commenced. Chaitanya sang and danced. He danced every evening for eight days during the 'Arati'. In the morning he would again perform 'Sankirtan' after bathing. During the rest of the time he swam in the Indrayumna Lake and performed water sports with his companions. After Jagannath was installed again in the main temple Chaitanya sang daily and recited verses in the Lord's praise.

When the Lord Krishna's birth festival 'Janmashtami' came king Pratarudra, Kashi Misra, Sarvabhaum joined Chaitanya in the dance. Chaitanya imitated a milkman by playing the role expertly with a stick as milkman are prone to do. Then his companions played the role of monkeys on the Vijayadshmi day (Dussera).

By this time four months had elapsed to the devotees from Bengal staying in Puri with Chaitanya and it was time they departed back home. Chaitanya gave Nitai (Nityananda) some instructions. Though they were secret, Chaitanya's biographers claim that these contained directions as to how to organise the Vaishnava sect.

Visit to Vrindavan via Bengal:

Chaitanya always wanted to visit Vrindavan but he was prevented repeatedly by his well wishers' advice. After he had taken 'Sannyasa' he wanted to settle in Vrindavan but in deference to his mother's wish he chose to settle in Puri. But after having stayed for so many months in Puri the urge to visit Vrindavan was again felt by him. King Prataprudra, however, felt that if he went away he wouldn't come back to Puri: so took counsel with Sarvabhuma and Ramananda to prevent him from leaving. The two disciples persuaded the master to stay on till autumn to be able to see the car festival. This appealed to Chaitanya and he agreed. Thereafter they said that it would be very cold in Vrindavan country and it might be better to go after Dol Yatra (around Holi), at the end of winter. Chaitanya again agreed. Meanwhile, a number of pilgrims came from Bengal. After they left Chaitanya expressed a desire to go to Bengal to see his mother. Thereafter he would go to Vrindavan. At the request of Sarvabhauma and Ramananda, he spent the rainy season in Puri and set out on his journey on the Vijayadashmi day. King Prataprudra made all arrangements for the journey through Orissa. At the boundary of Orissa the royal officer cautioned Chaitanya saying: 'Before you is the land of a wine-imbibing Moslem King through fear of whom no one travels on the road."

A spy of the Muslim king conveyed the news of Chaitanya's arrival. The spy and another messenger of the king, however, were so affected by the saint's sight that they began to chant the name of Krishna and continued chanting it before the king too. The Muslim governor who went, then, himself to the sage said: "Why didn't the fate send me as a Hindu to the earth? Then I would have come closer to thy feet" and started demanding end of his life. However, the governor got Chaitanya safely across the river.

Chaitanya did not visit Nawadweep this time and went straight to Shantipur to stay with Advait fro some time. There he also met Shachi, his mother. By this time Chaitanya's fame had reached far and wide. After few days stay and Shantipur he started going to Vrindavan as planned. But such a huge concourse of the people (devotees) followed him that he was advised not to go to Vrindavan with such a huge throng of people lest their intention should he mistaken. It seems the sage stayed in Bengal for about two months before he returned to Puri in the autumn. He stayed in Puri for some more time – some accounts say four month during the rainy season and left for Vrindavan in autumn.

But he took the difficult road to upper India. He had agreed to take with him a brahmin attendant called Balabhadra Bhattacharya to carry his belongings and to cook his food. Some accounts, particularly the "Chaitanya Charnamrita," give vivid details about Chaitanya's passing through the dense jungles he encountered on this path.

Chaitanya is described to have cast his voodoo of sorts on the land, jungles, trees and even the beasts. It is said that elephants, tigers, bears and herd of rhinoceros moved away from path at his sight. One day Chaitanya trod on a tiger by accident. In his abstraction he cried 'Speak Krishna!' and the tiger began to dance on its hind legs chanting 'Krishna!'. When Chaitanya sang the name of Krishna herds of bears came to listen and some tigers joined them. It is perhaps exaggeratedly claimed that the tigers and deer danced and embraced each other, chanting 'Krishna!'. The peacocks danced in ecstasy and so did other birds, even the trees and creepers rejoiced.

Finally he reached Kashi (Varanasi). There, while bathing at the Manikarnika Ghat Chaitanya met Tapan Misra, his old acquaintance who had been asked by Chaitanya himself to stay in Banaras during their previous meeting. Tapan invited the Chaitanya to stay with him. The sage (Chaitanya) visited Vindumadhava and Vishweshwara temples. He stayed at his house and would have his meals with Tapan. Though he had his old friend Chandrashekhar there he couldn't have had food with him because that fellow was not a brahmin. Then Banaras was the stronghold of the monists represented chiefly by Prakashananda Saraswati. He didn't take kindly to Chaitanya, and Chaitanya and his companions could not convince the headstrong monist. After staying ten days at Kashi, he left for Mathura. On the way he stayed at Allahabad for three days.

When he reached Mathura he prostrated himself in ecstasy of devotion. After bathing at Vishrant Ghat, he went to the Krishna temple and bowed at the image. He began to sing and dance in ecstasy. A brahmin joined him and a few people gathered there. The priest was convinced that Chaitanya was a young monk who had come to redeem them. The brahmin turned out to be a disciple of Madhavendra Puri who was the Guru of Ishwar Puri. As Ishwara was Chaitanya's preceptor, Chaitanya prostrated himself at the brahmin's feet. The brahmin showed him round the city and then they proceeded to Vrindavan.

As he proceeded towards Vrindavan from Mathura, Chaitanya seemed to be falling in a series of trances. It is said that the sage was so thrilled that he almost danced his way to Vrindavan. Dancing ecstatically he first reached the village Arith. There somewhat recovering his senses he asked as to where Radhakunda was. But nobody had heard about such a pool. But miraculously Chaitanya, believed to be Krishna himself in a fairer form, knew about it. And recollecting Krishna's act in the pool, he danced in rapture on the bank, painting his forehead with mud.

Thereafter he went to Sumanah tank. The sight of the Goverdhan hill threw him again in raptures. Then an interesting episode took place.

Being ardently desirous of seeing the image of Krishna Gopal which was in the temple at the top of the mount but he did not want to climb all the way up. While he was in this dilemma, in the night someone came with the news that he Turks were coming to plunder them that very night. Such raid were them a common feature. So out of fear the villagers left their homes the same night, carrying with them the image also. Then they went to a village called Gathooli. And next morning Chaitanya could have a 'Darshan' of Gopal at that village conveniently. After bathing in the Manasi Ganga Chaitanya went to see the Goverdhan hill which filled him with delight. While dancing he sang this verse from Bhagwata which meant. "O friends! Even this mount Goverdhan is the foremost among the servants of Lord Hari, for it delights at the touch of his feet and those of Balrama. It respects them and provides their cowherd friends and cattle with fish water, good gazing ground caves for shelter and edible sweet bulbs and roots."

Then Chaitanya visited various places in Vrindavana associated with Lord Krishna. Although the whole region remains ever instinct with love for Krishna and Radha, the then notable places were the Kamya forest, Nanddeshwar temple etc. After bathing in the 'pawan pool' he climbed the hillock and bowed to the image of Nanda and Yashoda and Krishna in between them. After dancing and singing there all day he visited the Khadir woods, Vishnu's image reposing on Sheshnag, Khel-teertha, the Bhandir and Bhadra woods, across the Yamuna, Shreevana, Lauhavana and the Mahavana which was Radha's birth place. After visiting Gokula he returned to Mathura. At Mathura he had to shift his residence from the Brahmin's house because of the large crowds, and went to Akrora-Ghat. From there he would frequently visit Vrindavan where he would perform the Sankirtan till mid-day. A rumour started doing rounds that Krishna was again showing forth at night and dancing on the hood of the serpent Kali, the snake. But it was all hoax. It was the fisherman's lights at Yamuna in the nights that gave this impression.

At times he used to be so much immersed in Krishna Bhakti (devotion to the Lord) that he would commit some dangerous acts also. One day while sitting on the Akroora Ghat he began to recollect that this was the place Akroora met Krishana and people got a glimpse of Gokula heaven. Moved day his thought he suddenly jumped into the river. Luckily Krishnadas and Balbhadra, his assistants were closeby who jumped behind him to drag him out of the water.

Apart from Chaitanya's uncontrollable emotional frenzy, other factor that was causing worry to his well-wishers were the swelling crowd every day. So they suggested Chaitanya to visit Prayag for the festival of Makar Sankranti. Although Chaitanya was loath to leave Vrindavana, he some how agreed to depart, perhaps in deference to their wishes.

Besides Balabhadra and Krishnadas three more devotees were with him when he left Mathura. On the way back he even converted Muslim soldiers into Krishna devotee. Reaching Allahabad (Prayag) he bathed at Sangam and remained 10 days there only.

On the way to Banaras (Kashi) from Allahabad (Prayag) he also met some Muslims who began to argue that there was just one God (monotheism) but Chaitanya refuted all his arguments. More than his arguments it was his style of saying 'Haribol!' and subsequent dance and music which used to spell-bind the onlookers. Same thing happened with these Muslims and 'bairagis' who later became famous as 'Pathan Vaishnavas'.

While at Vanarasi he also encounted the brothers

Rupa and Sanatana who had met Chaitanya earlier at Ramkali. It was at Kashi that Chaitanya helped them to get rid of their worldly illusions and concentrate their devotion on Lord Krishna.

However, the sannyasis (believers in the monism philosophy) denounced Chaitanya as they claimed that he spoke ill of them. The Marathi brahmin who was with Chaitanya thought the best way to stop this tirade of the monists would be to bring the Master and his denouncer together at one place. He was sure that they would come round once they fell under his charms. So Chandrashekhar, Tapan Misra and the brahmin persuaded Chaitanya to dine with the monists. Meanwhile on his way to the hosts house Chaitanya tarried at Vindu Madhava and began to dance in the Sankirtan manner along with his companions. A large crowd gathered there and their curiosity was awakened. Prakashananda, a leading monist, along with some other sannyasi came to see the 'dance' which they held so much in contempt. Seeing the leading monist Prakashananda and other sannyasi Chaitanya stopped dancing and bowed at them. Prakashananda and others also did the same. After exchanging some more compliments as befitted two such renowned adversaries, Chaitanya entered the meeting hall and bowed to all those that had assembled there, and sat in a corner. So impressed were the other sannyasis by Chaitanya's magnetic personality that they all stood up with Prakashananda requesting Chaitanya to come to the middle of the hall.

Then Prakashananda questioned him as to why being a saint he indulged in such cheap pranks as dancing and sankirtan and why didn't he study the Vedas. Chaitanya humbly replied: "I am ignorant and uneducated so my Guru instructed me to keep only chanting the name of Krishna". Thereafter Chaitanya went ahead to stress the virtue of Krishna's name and short comings in the Vedanta doctrine. Chaitanya's exposition of the Bhagwat's teaching so much impressed the Sannyasis that many of them instantly became his followers. This incident made Chaitanya famous in Banaras and it resulted in many monists starting study of the Bhagwat Purana. Thus even though he was unable to convert the monists, they look great interest in Vaishnavism. Subsequently, Chaitanya remarked in a lighter vein: "I came to sell emotionalism at Kashi but I find no takers. It doesn't sell and it is difficult to carry the load back home. You, too, were all sad at the idea that I should burden myself with this heavy load, so according to your wish I have distributed it here gratis". After this Chaitanya returned to Puri taking the short route as he had come by. It was about a year that he had been out of Puri this time.

VIII. His Last Days

Chaitanya's coming back to Puri rejoiced his followers to no end. When the news of his coming back from Vrindavan reached Nawadweepa his mother Shachi as overjoyed. They all rushed to meet him. Chaitanya enjoyed their company for about four months and then at his behest all the devotees from Bengal returned home. So long as Chaitanya was alive they thus kept making annual visits to Puri. Chaitanya himself also once thought of going to Bengal as many of his disciples were in no position to visit Puri. But as it happened the visits never materialised. During this period he wrote two plays 'Lalita-Madhava' and 'Vidagdha-Madahva' which were also read out before a gathering of prominent persons and they were greatly applauded.

By now Chaitanya fame had reached all parts of India with scores of people coming to see him at Puri. Chaitanya met them all very lovingly and bestowed this special blessings on those whom he thought worthy of it.

In Bengal Nitai (Nityananda) was his main disciple who spread Vaishnavism in Bengal. The 'Chaitanya-Charnā mrita' claims that whenever Nitai danced or did the Sankirtan in the house of Shachi or other houses, Chaitanya would always be mystically present there.

However Chaitanya had become rather hard on women in his last days. There is an incident related to 'Chota-Haridas' which merits elaboration.

One day Chaitanya was invited by Bhagwana Acharya, a great Vaishnava for meals at the later's house. As good quality of rice was not available, he called Chhota-Haridas who used to chant Lord Krishna's name in the Kirtans to bring a mound of white rice from the sister of Shipli Mahiti, Madhavi Devi, who was an old anchorite and devout Vaishnava. Praising the rice Chaitanya asked his host from where it had been got. The Acharya told him that Chhota-Haridas had obtained it from Madhavi. Chaitanya did not say anything, but on returning home asked Govinda never again to admit Haridas in his presence. The punishment was, doubtless, severe. None the less despite many pleas from his close associates like Damodar, Chaitanya did not relent. He told Damodar in very clear terms. "I can't look at a Vairagi (an anchorite averse to sensual attractions) who speaks to a woman. Our passions are hard to control and take hold of their natural objects of gratification. Even the wooden statue of a woman can steal the heart of an ascetic."

It was during these days that Chaitanya also cured Sanatan – his disciple who was left in Vrindavan and Mathura to spread Gandia-Vaishnavism by the Master. When Sanatan returned once to Puri to see his master he also came via the Jharkhand route and happened to catch a filthy skin disease making his body full of pustules. Not withstanding his filthy and contagious disease Chaitanya embraced him even when Sanatan asked him to remain away. One day Sanatan was coming to meet him, taking the longer route by the sea-shore to avoid meeting pious people and the circumventing deities images getting defiled by his presence. Chaitanya was touched by Sanatan's sincerity, saying. "Your touch can even purify even the gods and sages." And then Chaitanya lovingly embraced Sanatan. And lo and behold Sanatan's all blisters healed up in trice, making his body shine with a golden hue. The miracle was witnessed by many. Following this incident Sanatan proceeded to Vrindavan, Chanting Krishna's name and singing Chaitanya's praise all the way.

Chaitanya's Meeting Vallabhacharya :

It was about this time that Vallabhacharya came to

meet Chaitanya. Despite the two being totally different in personality – Vallabha proud of his scholarship while Chaitanya's anchor was only overpowering love for Lord Krishna – Vallabha kept Chaitanya in high esteem since he once saw Chaitanya dancing before Jagannath's chariot. In fact Chaitanya's dance was replete such 'rasa' as made the most erudite scholar forget their wisdom and prudence. Vallabha was so impressed with Chaitanya's devotion that as the latter left the former requested the former's companions to initiate him. Galadhar, Chaitanya's pet disciple, refused because he knew that the Master won't like it since Chaitanya's dislike for monists (at that time most of the learned scholar were influenced by Monism). Then Vallabha insisted on Chaitanya listening his commentary on the 'Bhāgwat'. But Chaitanya said he was not competent to listen to such a learned discourse. When Vallbha argued that he had made an unprecedented interpretation on Krishna's name, Chaitanya simply said: "I pay no regard to other interpretations. Krishna who is Yashoda's son and dark as the 'Taamal' leaves is my Lord and his name is enough knowledge for me." Then Vallabha tried to read out his commentary to Chaitanya's companion but they wouldn't either listen. Next day Vallabha went to meet Advaita to hold discussion. But Advaita refuted effectively all his arguments and Vallabha had to admit his defeat. One day Vallabha addressed Advait to the question. "Mankind is feminine and Krishna their husband is what you believe. But no (Indian) wife takes the name of her husband[1]. Yet you take Krishna's name?" Advait pointed out that the Master was sitting and he would answer the query. Chaitanya replied non-challantly. "A true wife obeys her husband's commands. Our husband has commanded us to chant his name ceaselessly. No true wife can disobey his command and so we chant his name and derive from it the fruit of love for Krishna's feet."

Though mightily impressed Vallabha was he was also baffled as to why the sage so nice to others was rather unhappy with him. Then he realised that perhaps his arrogance of possessing high knowledge had deterred his affection from reaching him. So he begged Chaitanya's forgiveness and thanked him for pointing out his shortcoming. Thenceforth he became an ardent devotee of Chaitanya and a devoted Vaishnava.

Chaitanya's Last Phase and the End :

Chaitanya, as his age advanced, became more and more prone to relapsing in the trance. He had also cut down on his food – although to prove that he was not

Believed to be indecent all ill-mannerly by traditional India ethos.

enamoured of comfortable living – and started having occasional bouts of illness. He had also asked the Bengali devotees always visiting him from the Bengal to cease coming to him with the parting fare-well address: "Every year you come here to see me undergoing many hardships on the journeys. For this reason I feel inclined to forbid your coming, but the pleasure of your society tempts my heart."

"I had commanded Nityananda to live in Bengal. He has come here in difference of my order, what can I say to him? The (old) Advait Acharya, leaving his wife, children and home behind, performs a long and difficult journey to meet me. How can I repay the debt of his love? I merely sit here at Nilachala (Puri) without having to do any exertion for your sake. I am a sannyasi, without wealth. With what shall I repay my debt to you? My only property is my body, and this I give up to you. Sell if you like!" Everyone there was moved at Chaitanya's words, and tears ran down their cheeks. Chaitanya also wept. They could not hear to leave him, and stayed on five or six days more at Puri. They left, bitterly unhappy. Chaitanya, too, was sad at heart.

Although Chaitanya was getting increasingly withdrawn from the world about this time, his purely humane considerations had not yet deserted him. The following incident reveals his considerate nature for his disciples.

Once Jagadananda had gone to Nawadweep to enquire about Shachi's condition. When he returned Shachi sent with him a medicated sandal oil's pot for Chaitanya. She had heard that Chaitanya was having frequent disturbance in his bile, wind and phlegm humours due to ill-health. She sent the oil for her son for massaging his body with it. But Chaitanya said: "A sannyasi is forbidden to use oil, particularly scented oil. Present it to the temple where it would be used to oil lamps, and thereby Jagadananda's labours will be rewarded." When Govinda persisted, the Master said in anger : " Very well, engage a masseur also to rub it! Is it for this kind of pleasure that I have taken Sannyas? Everyone will make fun of me and say: 'there goes a pleasure loving sannyasi?" Next morning when jagadananda came, Chaitanya said: "Pandit, you have brought me oil from Benagal. But being a sannyasi I can't accept it. Present it to the temple to light the lamp. "The Pandit said, "who told you this lie? I have brought no oil from Bengal." Saying so he brought the pot from his room and threw it on the floor, where it broke, spilling the oil. Then he rushed to his room and bolted the door and remained there without taking any food. When three days passed thus, Chaitanya went to Jagadananda's room and said: "Rise Pandit! You must cook food yourself for me. I will come at noon to eat it." Jagadananda cooked the meal and served it on banana leaves at the proper time. Chaitanya was all praise for the vegetable soup, and went on eating much beyond his normal appetite in his eagerness to please Jagadananda. After meals the Master went back to his house, but slept only when Govinda assured him that Jagadananda had eaten and broken his self – imposed fast. This incident highlights Chaitanya's love for his companions and aversion to worldly and sensual pleasures.

Although Chaitanya still took part in dancing at the chariot festival and cleaning the temple and its precincts, falling health and advancing age had started taking their lot out of him . Yet, undaunted he would get up before sunrise and go to the temple of Jagannath . Till his pet assistant Haridas's life time he would go with him. Thereafter he would recite Krishna's name for several hours. So particular he was about this that he would not accept food from anyone who did not recite Krishna's name at least a lakh times a day i.e. for about two to two and half hours a day. Though he liked good food he changed this habit in the later years. He had grown vehemently opposed to any luxury, and slept in very small room, his bed being the ribs of banana leaves. Once his companion

Jagadananda, seeing that the hard ribs hurt his emaciated body, prepared a cotton matters and a pillow and dyed them in saffron, But Chaitanya did not like it and on yet another companion, Damodar's pointing out that Jagadananda would be hurt if he refused the gift, he blurted out. "Then bring me a bedstead also. I cannot enjoy these pleasures any more as I am wedded to asceticism. I should sleep on the bare earth." Curbing his preferences he lived a strict and absentenious life following all the regulations prescribed by scriptures for Sannyasa.

Now Chitanya's falling in trances or having temporary communion with Krishna were increasing in frequency. He began to experience grief of the kind the Gopis had experienced when Krishna departed to Mathura. At times he sang and danced as though madness had taken possession of him. It was becoming increasingly difficult for him to sleep. It had become his habit to keep on chanting Krishna's name while awake.

One day his disciple Swarupa noticed total silence from his room in the depth of night, Taking a companion along Swarupa went out to search him, and found him lying near the lion gate of the temple. His arms and legs were without flesh and his hands, feet, neck and waist disjointed from the trunk and covered with bare skin. The devotees were alarmed and began to chant Krishna's name in his ears. After a while he cried 'Hari Bol!' and his body was restored as before.

Thus Chaitanya's last days were spent in half awakened and half-lost to the world state. Almost all the time he appeared lost in the vision of Krishna, Radha and Gopis. He appeared plunged in the ocean of grief of separation from Krishna. At times he would rave like a mad man, at time weep, then run here and there, roll on the ground and fall into a swoon.

Once on the full moon night of Vaishakh (April 15 to May 15) the Master went with his devotees to visit the great Jagannath – Vallabha park. The trees and creepers were in full bloom as it was spring. The night threw Chaitanya into a swoon. Then he asked the devotees to sing stanzas of the Geeta govinda.

> 'Soft sandal mountain – winds caress quivering veins of clove;
>
> Forest huts hum with droning bees and crying cuckoos.
>
> When spring's mood is rich Hari roams here
>
> To dance with young women, friend –
>
> A cruel time for deserted lover!

One day the Master said to his disciples. "The supreme healer in this Kali-age is Sankirtana. It enables one to conquer sin and it purifies soul. It leads us to devotion. You should chant Krishna's name everywhere, while working, at meals or in bed. It is omnipotent and not bound by time and space. The devotee should consider himself lowly as grass, whatever may be his position in life. He should be like a tree that does not cry when cut, nor begs for water when drying up. But, on the contrary, gives protections to all who ask, and bearing sun and rain itself protects others from them. However, highly placed, the vaishnava should eschew pride. He should venerate all forms of life as Krishna. Take Krishna's name and it will inspire you with love."

Chaitanya could experience his end coming nigh. When Advait left for Bengal he is said to have confided in him about his approaching end.

One day when dancing at the Vijaya of the car festival in the month of Ashadh his left toe was suddenly pierced by a brick lying on the road. On the sixth day of the moon the pain in his toe grew severer and he was forced to lie in the garden he had gone to with his disciples. Here he hold Pandit Goswami that he would leave the earth next night at 10 p.m. and so it happened. Nityananda consoled the disciples and vowed before them that they all should make every one a devotee of Krishna without differentiating any human being from others. And with this pledge from his disciples Chaitanya quitted his mortal coil to be one with his ultimate Lord, Lord Krishna.

IX. Chaitanya's Teachings and Related Literature

It must be made clear at the very outset that Chaitanya composed almost no book or tome worth the name himself though there are many books that are written on him. However, one poem : Ay re Jagai Madhai ay Hari name matbi jadi ay," is said to be his own creation though there are doubt about it as well. In a book published by National Book Trust, New Delhi, by Dilip Kumar Mukherjee, there is a poem in Sanskrit entitled : Shikshashtak' whose translation in English is given below:

i) Making the mind clean as a mirror, putting out the conflagration of worldliness, spreading goodness like the moon's light, Bride of wisdom and bliss, nectar of joy, victorious over the sneses – such is the 'Sankirtana' of Krishna.

ii) Your might is contained in your many names you are remembered by them for ever and ever, Such, O Lord, is your benedictions – But ah! Poor me I am bereft of your love.

iii) Be humble as a straw, forbearing as a tree Esteem other without caring for your repute.

iv) I desire neither wealth, nor might nor lovely girls,
Nor the gift of poetry, O Lord of the universe,
I only desire to be your devotee
Life after life.

v) O son of Nanda, Krishna,
Your servant is cast in this difficult ocean of life
Consider him to be a speck of dust
On your lotus feet.

vi) When will that day come
When a stream of tears flows from my eyes,
My voice is choked with emotion,
My body's hair stand on end?

vii) Says Radha when Krishna is away
A moment seems like an eon
My eyes rain tears
And all the world is a void.

viii) Says Radha, whether Krishna crushes me
To his bosom,
Or leaves me miserable by going away,

Or sports with other girls,
He alone is the Lord of my life.

The Concepts Chaitanya Adhered to :

(a) The concept of Difference in Non-Difference:

This philosophy of Gaudiya – Vaishnavism to which Chaitanya adhered is termed in Sanskrit as 'Bhedabheda' i.e. the inscrutable relationship between difference and non-difference. This school believed in Brahman (Supreme Being) but didn't conceive of it as something incomprehensible. When Maitreya asked Parashara as to how could creative energy be attributed to Brahman if we take it to be 'unqualified' (Nirgun), Parashara told him that it was like heat arising from fire. (Vide 'the Vishnu-purana'). This problem of creation arising from impersonal Brahman was solved by saying that it is incomprehensible to thought. Shridhar Goswami – a Chaitanya school follower – defined this concept as that which is not open to logical proof and is self-evident.

However, this concept of difference in non difference is explained best by Sanathan Goswami – as that of the sea and the wave. The wave is part of the sea, but not the sea itself. The sea is much vaster and consists of many other things – like, coral, acquatic creatures, sea-plants etc, which the waves may never have. The difference between the believers of the Advait concept and the Bhedabhed concept is that while the former believe only the sea to be real not the wave, the latter believes that since wave is part of the same reality (sea) it has to be real. Anything unreal can't be created from real no matter it may appear beyond realisation. The followers of Chaitanya claim that this perception can only be realised through soul like Bhakti but never understood by knowledge.

(b) The World is not an Illusion:

Perhaps this is a logical corollary of the belief of 'Bhedabhed'. The followers of this belief – the school of Gandiya Vaishnavism refute the idea: "Brahma Satya jaganmithya" and claim that 'Jagat' (world) is not an illusion. They argue that if it was illusory or non-existent what would be the purpose of human endeavour which beings make to realise themselves. When emancipation is achieved, the world is not destroyed. Only the illusory notions are no more Brahman.

(c) Brahman:

In the school of Vaishnavism which Chaitanya also adhered to, Brahman is eternal i.e. without beginning or end, infinite and all pervading. Chaitanya called him Krishna, Vasudeva, Vishnu and Narayan, He believed that Shiva and other deities are only Krishna's manifestations. But they are not so perfect in powers and attributes. Therefore they are said to be 'swansh' (subjective portions) of Krishna and totally dependent on him, while Krishna is self-dependent. Thus to Chaitanya, Krishna is supreme. He identified him with Brahman. But he believed that this Brahman had human form also. Krishna alone is 'Sat-Chit-Ananda', 'Sat' (truth) because he exists and upholds the existence of others; 'Chit' because he knows and makes others know, and 'Ananda' because he is pure bliss. While all 'shaktis' (divine power) remain dormant in Brahman, in Bhagwat (human embodiment of Brahman) all these Shaktis are activate.

(d) Jiva (the Soul) :

The Gandiya-Vaishnava belief was that jiva (soul) and Brahman (Supreme Being) are not identical but there is a bond of love between them. According to Chaitanya Ishwar (God) is like a roaring fire and the souls are sparks issuing from it. They are atomic in size and infinite. Explaining there various natures to Sanatana Goswami, Chaitanya said that they are of two kinds. The first are freed souls which are ever free and the second those which are ever in bondage. Explaining their distinction further he said that the souls 'which are free are devoted to God from eternity. They are not under Maya's (divine illusion's) influence i.e. they are not deluded and enjoy the grace of God. The souls is bondage have turned away from God and so not enjoying his Grace. They are the ones that have to be awakened by their follow souls by making them devoted to God the rough various means like devotion, Sankirtan etc. They have to be driven away from worldly pursuits.

e) Emancipation (Mukti or Moksha) :

This sect believes that emancipation can be got both in life itself, as well after death. When the true nature of God is realised, the false concept one may have had about Him Vanishes, that is emancipation. It must be understood that emancipation is always of the soul and never of the body. And for soul death has no meaning. For soul is beyond emancipation at any stage. Whether in life or in death. So emancipation is achieved when in soul and God relationship the celebrated 'Asampragyats-Yoga' or the union of coalescence is achieved.

Moreover, knowing is reckoning distinctively. But in union of coalescence where is no separation, no more distinctive identities. When all bear One identity where is the difference? As "Kāmāyani" creator, the ace modern Hindi poet Jayashankar Prasad proclaimed in his magnum opus of this name "Sab pahichance lagte the; Apnee hee ek kala se!" [All looked recognised is one, phase of their own oneness." (translation by the author).

It is to that union of coalescence that Chaitanya preached and aspired for – and going by some of the available accounts – achieved it himself.

It won't be incongruous if the term for devotion in Sanskrit is dwelt on a hit in this concept. Bhakta or devotee's one root in Sanskrit is also from division. That which has been divided or separated from the parent whole is Bhakta and his or her entire life's endeavour is always guided by the motivation force of union or coalescence. The purport of Chaitanya's teaching, as also conveyed the creations by the Goswamis (given ahead) is that both knowledge and words must awaken Bhakti for Krishna. If they don't do that, they do not have much use. Then end obtained by the yogis by following the path 'raja-yoga', namely "Chitli-Vrittinirodha" (the freezing or destruction of the mind's modulations) is effortlessly obtained by the devotee. In Bhagwat Gita the Lord mentions that there are three paths open before an aspirant : that of Knowledge, that of Action, that of Devotion. The Bhakti-school followers including Chaitanya always maintained that of devotion is easiest to pursue but what it needs is total and unwavering concentration or the immersion of self in that pursuit.

And Chaitanya had achieved it. As D.C. Sen, one of the biographers of Chaitanya, described about Chaitanya's this emancipation, so must be deemed to be Chaitanya's own concept about emancipation. "Every sound to him conveys to him a sense divine presence and every touch the warmth of divine contact. The devotee attains to a state of frenzy. The Lord's approach, the dark blue sky, the sea and the landscape became symbolic of the colour of divine figure."

Perhaps Chaitanya's this concept of emancipation was also the Sufi concept. May be, the Muslim theological influence had become rather influential in Chaitanya's age also since this feeling of oneness is also described by 'Ghalib' in a similar thought-wave"

"Asle-shuhood-e-shaahide-mashahood ek hain
Hairan hoon phir mushahida hai kis hisaab men?"

[When the viewer, the view and the viewed are one who is observing whom?]

f) Chaitanya and the Sankirtana Tradition:

'Kirtan' literally means singing praise or glory of some divine personage. Sankirtana means a kind of 'Choir-singing' where in a large group sings one song or even one line together 'Sam' is a prefix in Sanskrit which literally means more than one. So Sankirtan is a group singing. In fact in Sankirtana only one line the burden is infinitely repeated. Like "Hare Rama Hare Krishan; Krishna Krishna, Hare Hare. It is believed that when a devotee repeats endlessly one's chosen deity's name, some sort of communion is established between the deity and the devotee. It was found to be more engrossing way to keep on repeating one's chosen god's name, rather than plainly pronouncing it unmusically. Music, particularly Indian Music, is believed to generate an atmoshphere most conducive to concentration. Even pure notes are supposed to spell-bound not only the human beings but even animals. There are scores of such tails as describe how Tansen could captivate even the deers. Since Indian Music is melody based it has greater power of enchantment than the western music which is harmony-based.

Why Chaitanya chose blending of music in his style of worship is because Bengal even otherwise, has a rich musical heritage-Vishnupur, not far from Nawadweepa has been an age old centre of music in Bengal. Chaitanya was naturally influenced by the prevailing belief and in order to derive greater concentration to visualise his Supreme Lord, Krishna, he very melodiously blended music in his devotion. Perhaps he was inspired by Jayadeva, the celebrated poet and singer who existed three hundred years before Chaitanya.

But what differed Chaitanya's style of worship from that the Jayadeva was Chaitanya's emphasing only chanting the name of the chosen deity in groups with melodious music. Now this sort of worship requires no particular qualification, no knowledge even of music – but only unbound devotion for the Lord. Although this style of musical devotion was quite popular in north India during the medieval period when Mira-bai and Surdas were spell-bending the generations, to Chaitanya alone goes the credit of popularising 'the Sankirtan tradition'.

Infact it was Chaitanya who invented the peculiar form of chanting Krishna's name accompanied by the 'Pakhaavaja' (a kind of drum) and 'Kartals' (a kind symbals which synchronise their beat with each other. It was Chaitanya's 'Sankirtan' which carried the message of Krishna Bhakti to common people in far flung distant villages. It required only two simple musical instruments and religious fervour to make itself effevtive. It was again Chaitanya who also introduced a new element – dancing, while chanting the holy name. So he is looked upon as the originator of this kind of especial worship which is still popular through many similar movements, the most renowned being the Hare Rama Hare Krishna Movement.

It is said that king Prataprudra the ruler of Puri was captivated by Chaitanya Mandali's Sankirtan. Once he asked his court's pundit as to what kind of music it was. The Pandit, Sarvabhaum, told him. "It has been created by 'Chaitanyadeva." Chaitanya used to become so overpowered by his devotion to Lord Krishna that he used to feel utterly helpless to do anything else but chant his Lord's name. It is claimed by his biographers that when the devotees of Nawadweepa came to pay homage to Chaitanya he advised them to sing tune. "Hare Krishna, Hare Krishna, Krishna Krishna, Hare Hare'. Of course apocryphally, but it is said that Chaitanya himself composed a shloka (verse) in which he explained how the holy name should be uttered.

"A devotee who chants the holy name ought to be humbler than a blade of grass, more forbearing than a tree, free from lust and anger despite provocation, content with what he has, not avaracious and giving due honour to others without desiring it himself. While chanting God's name one should always bear this in his mind."

Thus Chaitanya went about singing the name of Krishna in a huge concourse of people. Later, after Chaitanya's death, when the 'padas' and 'shrotras' were composed these were set to tune and sung in the mode of Kirtana. This kind of music came to be known as 'Padavali Kirtana'. The 'Padavali Kirtana' was introduced at the festival held on the bank of the Padma river at Khetari in Rajshahi district, at the instance of Narottamdasa in the mid eighties of the sixteenth century. This became known as 'garanhati' or 'garerhati' type of Kirtana – perhaps because Khetari was situated in the Garera Hat paragana. Vishnupriya, Chaitanya's window was present at Kherati Sankirtana Samaroha. It was Narottamdas who introduced the singing of Kirtana in the classical Dhruvapada style. There were two parts in this Kirtana: the alaapa and the neivedya. All those versed in music know that alaapa is generally not accompanied by any 'Taal' or beat since it is free singing. Then comes neivedya or the wordy offerings. In other words alaapa is meant for creating the atmosphere while 'nivadha' (Naivadya) is the actual request to the Lord.

The 'padavali kirtana' continued in Bengal as a significant form of music upto the mid-eighteenth century, but from 19th century onwards it started to fade out. It was revived a few decades back by the Hare Rama Hare Krishna Movement or by the ISKCON movement. Some scholars claim that this was also the inspiration behind Rabindra Nath Tagore creating his style of music: 'Rabindra Sangeeta.'

There is no doubt that this unique musical innovation by Chaitanya had wide-spread influence in a large part of upper India. Chaitanya's name is inseparably linked with Sankirtana.

(g) The Gosains (Goswamis) : The Carrier of Chaitanya Tradition and Creation of Literature on Chaitanya:

The term Goswami is associted with those who have won over the temptation of the sensual delights. 'Go' in Sanskrit means senses or 'Indriya'. And those who have mastered them are called Goswami. The popular Medieval Hindi Poet, Goswami Tulsidas is also accredited with this title. However, the Gosains who carried forward Chaitanya tradition and wrote copiously on Chaitanya are slightly different group. They were generally the priests in various temples and influenced by Chaitanya style of Bhakti started writing poems and 'pada' to be sung at the Sankirtan concerts. These Gosains wrote many celebrated philosophical works in Sanskrit. The Prominent among them already referred to in the narration earlier were Rupa, Sanatan, Raghunathdasa, Bhatta, Gopal Bhatta and Jiva. Chaitanya himself had assigned Rupa and Sanatana, the two brothers, to write an account of Vaishnava faith according to the direction given to him. Their nephew Jiva helped them in the task. These three-Rupa, Sanatana and Jiva – were, apart from saints and ascetics theologians, poets and men of literary accomplishments. Gopal Bhatta was associated with them.

These Gosains acquire prominent place in Chaitanya literature because, since not much of Chaitanya's original creation in verse or prose is available, the literature by these Gosains on Chaitanya throws much light on Chaitanya own thinking , belief and life-style. The Gosains of Vrindavan owe their origin to these Gosains, though they had their own contribution in the tradition of the Sankirtan started by Chaitanya, also called Gaurang (white or fair complexioned) Mahaprabhu (super lord).

We have already given the gist of the rendering in English of the text believed to be Chaitanya's own compositions. But given below are the selected renderings of what are believed to be these Gosains contributions in

Chaitanya literature. First set of Shlokas are from Rupa Goswami's composition in Sanskrit entitled: "Shri Shri Namastakam."

1. O Hari! your lotus feet are lit up by the light of the Vedas
   You are adored by liberated souls, I take refuge in you.

2. All hail! you whose names saints chant, who gives eternal bliss
   You appear as the world, you destroy the acute suffering of those
   Who even chant the shadow of your name.

3. The sun of your blessed name dispels the darkness of ignorance
   From the minds of those steeped in worldliness,
   It brings devotion to those who are blind to the light within
   Who can sing all your glories? There is no end to them.

4. Even constant meditation on the Absolute cannot destroy the seeds of birth,
   But the chanting of Hari's name destroys them, so say the Vedas.

5. O Slayer of demon Agha! O son of Yashoda and

Nanda
O Lotus-eyed, O! Moon of the gopis, O Lord of Vrindavana!
You are compassionate to the submissive O Krishna, of many forms;
May I be devoted to you for ever.

6. O holy Lord! You are personal as well as impersonal.
But to us dearer is your more compassionate personal form,
Because when we, the offending fallen souls, chant it,
We are submerged in the blissful ocean of divine love.

7. O holy Lord! You wash away the sins of your devotees
Who take refuge in your lotus feet; you are the light of bliss
O Krishna, holy lord of Gokula, O divine from!
I humbly bow to you again and again.

8. O divine nectar of love, O Lord Krishna your name comes alive in Narada's vina
I beseech you, O Lord, make me ever sing of your divine love.

The second set of the eight Shlokas is also from Rupa Goswami. In these set of verses Rupa Goswami hails Shree Chaitanya as the Lord and Master Himself. These verses are also called. Invocation to the Saint.

May I see Shri Chaitanya again,
Who is greatly loved
By gods who incarnate themselves,
Who teaches his bhaktas the nature of devotion.

May I see Shri Chaitanya again,
The comfort of saints in their distress,
Graceful to his devotees,
Filled with divine love like that of the maids of Vraja.

Who is the support of Damodara Swarupa,
Loved by Advaita Prabhu, venerated by Pandita,
Who has glorified Parmananda and redeemed Thakura,
And bestowed his blessings on Gajapati.

May I see him again who is drunk with Krishna's love,
Of beauty a million times that of Kama
The diadem of saints: clothed like the crimson dawn,
Of saffron limbs outvying molten gold.

The names of Hari, Krishna and Rama ever on his tongue,
His bright left hand holding the rosary dangling to his waist,
Long eyes reaching his ears, arms hanging to his knees-
I long to see Shri Chaitanya thus, again.

May I see him again filled with divine love,
Swooning with the remembrance of Vrindavana
And of the groves along the riverside,
His nimble tongue ever chanting the name of Krishna.

Would that I saw Shri Chaitanya again
Dancing in ecstasy out of love for Krishna,
While before Lord Jagannath's car bound for Sundarachala,
The vaishnava throng thrills with chanting Krishna's name.

The stream of whose tears seems to wash away the earth,
Overwhelmed with ecstasy in the chanting throng
Whose hair stand on end as the stamens of the 'kadamba'
Whose limbs glisten with beads of perspiration.

May divine love issuing from Shri Chaitanya's lotus feet
Flood the heart of the fortunate one
Who daily recites with constant devotion

These bliss-giving eight verses that sing his qualities and deeds.

The following set of verses are culled from Rupa Goswami's "Shree Shree Upadeshaamritam'. The English rendering is by D.K. Mukherjee.

He who is free from anger and lust
Who does not prattle idly, who does not speculate,
Who's not a glutton or a gourmandizer,
That man of controlled senses is master of the earth.

Acquisitiveness, frivolous pursuits, vain talk and evil company
Bondage to rules and indifference to truth – these destroy devotion.

Enthusiasm, certitude, patience, observance of rites,
Shunning evil company and saintliness – these are the sings of devotion.

Giving and accepting for the Lord, spiritual talk and discussion,
Feeding the saints and partaking of their leavings- these are the signs of devotion.

Look favourably on him who chants Krishna's name
To him who serves Krishna with single-minded devotion prostrate yourself,
But be friend and listen wholeheartedly to one
Who is above cynicism and serves the Lord with inner devotion.

Pure is the sincere devotee even though imperfect of habits and limbs
The Ganga water remains sacred despite its muddiness and foam.

Ignorance goes away only by chanting Krishna's name
As it is the taking of sugar candy which cures biliousness.

The tongue chanting the holy name, the mind dwelling to Mathura,
Contemplating the sports of Krishna, the devotee should dwell in Vraja.

Mathura is superior to Vaikuntha, Vrindavana to Mathura,
Goverdhana is superior to Vrindavana and superior to Goverdhana is Radha Kunda;
Who is the devotee who will not render service
To the divine couple of Radha Kunda on the slopes of Goverdhana?

In order of ascending importance come-the men of works;
The men of knowledge; the devotees; the Krishna devotees;
The milkmaids of Vraja; and even more Radha
Who is the person who will not take refuge in her lotus feet and her Kunda?

Radha-Kunda is the symbol of intense love of Krishna for Radha,
It is superior to devotional works, so the sages declare;
When it confers divine love even on ordinary bathers
How much more on the devotees who bathe in it?

Raghunath Goswami wrote a set of verses in each of which he addressed the mind to immerse itself in Krishna's devotion. This set of verses is entitled; 'Manah-shiksha' and contains eleven verses, with a verse at the end setting forth the reward of one who chants aloud these verses. A sampled English version is given below:

1. O Mind, abandon all thoughts of egoin and worldliness
And dwell on the milkmaids of Vraja with staunch devotion,
On the spiritual hymns of the Master, the holy name of Krishna
And upon the divine young couple of Vraja.

2. O Mind, care not for fruitless Vedas,
Render service to Radha-Krishna in Vraja;
Meditate constantly on Shachi's son
The divine Master. The lover one of Krishna.

3. Mind, if you ardently desire to serve the divine couple in Vraja
Life after life, then listen
Bow down with love to Shri Swarupa
To Shri Rupa and his followers and to Shri Sanatana.

4. O Mind, shun idle gossip which impedes service of Krishna,
Let not Mukti, the tigress, swallow your urge for devotion,
Covet not Vaikuntha by worshipping Lakshmi-Narayana,
But ever serve Radha-Krishna in Vraja and obtain divine love.

5. O Mind! vile deeds born of lust, anger and the like
Are like highway robber throttling to death the spiritual wayfarer,
Shout aloud for the help of the killer of Baka (a demon)
He will deliver you from their terrible hold.

6. O Mind, do you not see the ass hypocrisy
Why do you bathe in its urine and burn both yourself and me?
Bathe eternally in the ocean of divine dalliance of

Giridhara
And make both yourself and me happy.

7. O Mind, Vainglory dances in my heart like a dog-eating pariah woman
How then can it be blessed with holy love
Render service to Gurudeva who will save you from her
And shower on you the precious gift of Radha-Krishana's love.

8. O Mind, Krishna has created Vrindavana on earth for me,
Now forsake hypocrisy and go about singing his praise
Merciful Krishna will then graciously confer on you
Radha divine service consecrated with his love.

9. O Mind, medicate on the grove of Vraja
The Abode of Radha the Ruler of mu soul,
Mediate on the milkmaids Lalita and Vishakha
And Radha-Kunda and Goverdhana which please the holy pair.

10. O Mind, served Radha the loved one of Krishna,
Who casts into the shade the luster of Rati and Gauri,
Who has eclipsed the fortune of Lakshmi and

Satyabhama
And outdone the love of consorts like Chandravali.

11. O Mind, meditate steadfastly as a handmaid of Radha
Be as one of the confidantes to serve the holy paid,
Drink deep of the nectar of the holy service of Govardhana
Got by hearing, chanting and meditating on Krishna's holy name.

12. He who chants these eleven verses in a sweet voice
Considering himself to be a follower of Rupa Goswami,
Obains the gem of Radha-Krishna devotion in Gokula
Which is the end of all human existence.

Shri Vishwanath Chakravarti also wrote a set of eight verses ('Ashthak') in Praise of his Guru, Chaitanya, entitled: 'Shri Shri Gurvashthakam'. A simplified English rendering is given below :

1. I offer my obeisance's to the feet of my divine master
Who is like a cloud of mercy to put out the conflagration of worldliness.

2. I bow to him whose hair stand on end, who trembles
and sheds tears of joy
When Shri Chaitanya sings and dances whorshipping
the Lord.

3. I bow to the lotus feet of my master who ever serves
the holy image
And cleans the temple and induces the Lord's
devotees to do the same.

4. I bow to my master who distributes the offerings
made to the holy image,
To those devotees of the Lord who are pure of heart.

5. I bow humbly to the feet of my master who is eager
savour
Each moment the sports, attributes, forms and names
of Radha-Krishna.

6. I bow to the feet of my master who prompts the
maids of Vrindavana
In fruthering the amorous sports of the young pair in
the groves of Vraja.

7. I bow to the feet of my master whom devotees look
upon as divine
Of whom the scriptures say so too and who is the
Lord's most beloved.

8. I bow to my master whose grace alone confers the divine blessing
Without which there is no salvation; I meditate on him constantly and sing hymns in his praise.

9. He who with guilelessness and humility chants these verses at early dawn.
Will for certain serve the Lord on shedding his moral body.

"The world looks void without Krishna. Even if he gives me pain that would be my joy, for whatever he gives me like a loyal wife accepting any gift from her husband be it ill or be it good in the world's eyes-should always be accepted as bliss. I don't want anything for myself. Whatever he gives me is my joy be it pain or be it pleasure in the eyes of the world."